Access

To

The Anointing

Preparation For The
Impartation of Next Level Ministry

~Deluxe Classic Edition~

Dr. Michelle Corral

Dr. Michelle Corral

ISBN 978-0-9975864-7-3

Unless otherwise stated, all Scripture quotations are taken from the King James Version (KJV) of the Bible.

DEDICATION

This book is dedicated to the living legacy of Kathryn Kuhlman, the Apostle of the Holy Spirit whose ministry mentored thousands.

It is also dedicated to my loving husband, Reverend Manuel Corral, the love of my life. His uncompromising life has given me the strength to go forward.

Dr. Michelle Corral

TABLE OF CONTENTS

FOREWORD

Words cannot express how much the Lord has blessed my life and ministry through Dr. Michelle Corral. She is a true believer, intercessor and scholar of the Word. If anyone has been proven and qualified by the Lord to minister about His anointing, it is Michelle Corral. She is a powerful vessel and instrument of God's glory that is being released in the kingdom for such a time as this.

In this book, Dr. Corral explains the anointing in a way that is easy to understand and activate in your life. It is filled with nuggets of scripture and wisdom that you can easily take to your prayer closet or apply as you go about your daily routine.

Most importantly, if you take this message to heart you will draw closer to the Lord than ever before-and that is the place of divine refreshing and restoration.

In this hour, it is vital that you have an intimate relationship with God and know how to identify and operate within the anointing. So take some time, let Dr. Corral give you biblical instruction that will equip you for every good work. Read this wonderful study slowly and carefully. Read it from cover to cover as often as needed to saturate yourself in the truth of this message. God has a powerful destiny in store for you, and you will access it by way of the anointing.

Enjoy.

-Dr. Juanita Bynum

Dr. Michelle Corral

Prayer to the Holy Spirit for Access to the Anointing in Your Life

Holy Spirit breathe upon me. Awaken me to the anointing. I will pay any price to be a surrendered servant in Your hands. Teach me to yield to You. I claim a new sensitivity and surrender to You. Teach me how to flow and follow You. Today, I pray the prayer of John the Baptist. Help me decrease, so You can increase in my life (John 3:30). Make me like Jesus, who as a man, though completely God, surrendered His entire Self to You. As I pass through the Red Sea of my journey, take me to the place of Your power. Baptize me with a new anointing. I want to be Yours. Help me to know You as a person and not just a power. Glorify Jesus through me to everyone I meet. Release and increase access to the anointing in my life.

Chapter One

Seven Avenues Of Access

Perhaps there has been a moment in your Christian walk when you felt an undeniable touch from God and said to yourself, "What is happening? I've never experienced anything like this before!"

This may have taken place while you were quietly praying at home or during a church service when it seems you were lifted into the very presence of the Lord during a time of praise and worship.

A visitation from heaven doesn't have to be an isolated experience. I believe you can have the anointing of the Holy Spirit flowing within you continually.

On these pages I am going to share what God has revealed to me concerning this unique and treasured gift. I believe it will move you into a new dimension of your Christian life. I am often asked the question, "How can I come into God's

Dr. Michelle Corral

presence? What can I do to prepare myself to receive this touch of the Spirit?" *— reach inside, search x meaning*

Before we begin to delve into God's Word concerning what the Lord has in store for you, let me share the "anatomy of the anointing"---what it is and how it will affect your spiritual future. These are avenues you need to walk which give access to God's special touch on your life.

1. THE ANOINTING IS THE ABIDING PRESENCE AND POWER OF GOD

Chosen by divine selection

We are not talking of a once-in-a-lifetime event, but a daily, "abiding" presence of the Spirit---which is accompanied by God's truth and power.

Scripture tells us, "But the anointing which ye have received of him abideth in you, and ye need not that any man teach you: but as the same anointing teacheth you of all things, and is truth, and is no lie, and even as it hath taught you, ye shall abide in him " (1 John 2:27).

Think of it! You will have nonstop instruction in the things of God.

2. THE ANOINTING WILL GIVE YOU A COMMISSION FOR YOUR MISSION

When Saul was anointed to lead Israel, "...Samuel took a vial of oil, and poured it upon his head, and kissed him, and said, Is it not because the Lord hath anointed thee to be captain over his inheritance?" (1 Samuel 10:1).

Saul's future was now in God's hands. He was commissioned for a great mission!

If you lack a sense of vision and are searching for divine direction, ask the Lord to pour out His Spirit on your future.

3. THE ANOINTING BRINGS A FRESH REVELATION AND IMPARTATION OF GOD'S PRESENCE TO YOU

By its very nature, the anointing is never stale or old-always fresh and new.

MC+

By its nature, the anointing is never stale or old-always fresh and new.

I've met those who constantly live in the past, talking about what God did for them ten, fifteen, even twenty years ago. As wonderful as those blessings were, you cannot operate with oil which has lost its zest and vitality.

I pray you will be able to say with the psalmist, "I shall be anointed with fresh oil" (Psalm 92:10).

This is the secret to receiving a "now" revelation from the Lord.

4. THE ANOINTING BRINGS YOU INTO A RELATIONSHIP OF PERSONAL POSSESSION

When we become anointed, it changes the relationship we have with Almighty God. Suddenly, He considers us to be His personal possession.

Of course, everyone who receives Jesus as Savior belongs to Him, yet there is a certain affinity with the Lord which takes place through the anointing. You become absolutely separated from the world and are "His" alone. In the book of Psalms, we find this concept of "possession" expressed in scriptures which use personal pronouns. For example:

- ❖ God shows "…mercy to His anointed" (Psalm 18:50)
- ❖ The Lord "…saveth his anointed" (Psalm 20:6).
- ❖ "The kings of the earth set themselves…against the Lord, and against his anointed" (Psalm 2:2). The Lord "…is the saving strength of his anointed" (Psalm 28:8).
- ❖ The Almighty declares, "I have ordained a lamp for mine anointed" (Psalm 132: 17).

❖ "Behold. . .look upon the face of thine anointed "(Psalm 84:9).

❖ God warns, "Touch not mine anointed, and do my prophets no harm"(Psalm 105:15).

In each of these verses, God is assuring us, "When you receive My anointing, you are My personal possession."

This is not just for those called to full-time ministry, but for all believers who have the touch of God on their lives.

5. THE ANOINTING PREPARES YOUR PLATFORM IN THE PRESENCE OF YOUR ENEMIES

It does not matter what weapon is formed against you (Isaiah 54:15) or how the devil schemes to bring you down; through the anointing you are guarded and protected by God Himself.

> *MC+*
> *Through the anointing you are guarded and protected by God Himself.*

The psalmist declares, "Thou preparest a table before me in presence of mine enemies: thou anointest my head with oil; my cup runneth over"(Psalm 23:5).

The enemies who have been testing you may not be physical, but demonic in nature. But, praise God, when your head is anointed with oil, He prepares a "table"--a platform--regardless of the problems engulfing you.

6. THE ANOINTING BRINGS A DESIGN OF DELIVERANCE IN YOUR LIFE

There is something about the anointing that always brings the Yeshua – the Hebrew word for Jesus, the Messiah of the Old Testament.

This powerful name, Jesus, brings deliverance. Yes, "...thy name is as ointment poured forth" (Song of Solomon 1:3). There is anointing in His precious name. This is the same heavenly touch received by the Son of power of God. The Bible tells how the Father "...anointed Jesus of Nazareth with the Holy Ghost and with power: who went about doing good, and healing all that were oppressed of the devil; for God was with him"(Acts 10:38).

MC+

This is the mighty, bondage-breaking power of God.

This is the mighty, bondage-breaking power of God.

Here is a Messianic text which reveals how the revelation of the anointing is accompanied by the design of deliverance: "The spirit of the Lord God is upon me; because the Lord hath anointed me to preach good tidings unto the meek; he hath sent me to bind up the brokenhearted, to proclaim liberty to the captives, and the opening of prison to them that are bound" (Isaiah 61:1).

You can find total freedom from the grip of bondage over your finances, your body, your mind, your work or your marriage, by being under the flow of the anointing.

If you know someone who has a broken spirit, bring them into the place where God's heavenly oil is being outpoured. It will break the chains and set them free. "And it shall come to pass in that day, that his burden shall be taken away from off thy shoulder, and his yoke from off thy neck, and the yoke shall be destroyed because of the anointing" (Isaiah 10:27).

Thank God, you don't have to confront your problems alone. You have a yoke-breaker and a burden-lifter.

7. THE ANOINTING GIVES US ACCESS INTO THE ATMOSPHERE OF HEAVEN

Something miraculous happened to Jacob after his father, Isaac, pronounced the blessing of Abraham over him.

On a journey, tired, he found a place to sleep, using a Stone for his pillow. The Bible records how Jacob "...dreamed, and behold a ladder set up on the earth, and the top of it reached to heaven: and behold the angels of God ascending and descending on it" (Genesis 28:12).

In this revelation, Jacob saw the Spirit of the Father extending the boundaries from the home of God to planet earth. It gave him direct access into the atmosphere of heaven.

After this prophetic dream concerning Jacob's promised future, he said the place where he slept was "the house of God, and this is the gate of heaven" (v. 17).

Then, "...Jacob rose up early in the morning, and took the stone that he had put for his pillows, and set it up for a pillar; and poured oil upon the top of it" (v.18).

This was now sacred, holy ground-consecrated by the oil of anointing.

Are you ready to live in the atmosphere of heaven? In the next chapter I want to show you from God's Word how this glorious life is possible.

Chapter Two

Separated And Submitted

Even now, as you begin to read this book, I pray you are saying, "Yes, I am ready for the Lord to give me access into the atmosphere of heaven."

In this chapter I want to show you from God's Word what makes this possible and how it can become a glorious reality. When you open your heart to the Father's will, the boundaries of heaven will be enlarged and extended to you.

There are two divine principles involved:

FIRST:

THE ANOINTING SEPARATES FROM WHAT IS SECULAR

One of the important Hebrew concepts we need to understand is what has been called "forbidden mixture."

Just as oil and water do not mix, there is something about the anointing that separates itself from what is earthly or carnal. When the presence of God's Spirit is poured out, the secular must break away.

A great example of this is found in the tribe of Levi—one consecrates of the twelve tribes of Israel.

In the prophetic sense of Scripture, the Levites prefigure how the anointing separates and consecrates our service to God.

MC+

In the prophetic sense of Scripture, the Levites prefigure how the anointing separates and consecrates our service to God.

WHOLLY MINE FOR A DIVINE DESIGN

The book of Numbers derives its name from the fact that two years after the children of Israel began their exodus from Egypt, A national census was taken. God instructed Moses in the Tent of Meeting on the desert of Sinai, "Take ye the sum of all the congregation of the children of Israel, after their families, by the house of their fathers, with the number of their names, every male by their polls; From twenty years old and upward, all that are able to go forth to war in Israel: thou and Aaron shall number them by their armies" (Numbers 1:2-3).

However, there was one tribe which was excluded from this count. The Lord instructed Moses, "Only thou shalt not number the tribe of Levi, neither take the sum of them among the children of Israel: But thou shalt appoint the Levites over the tabernacle of testimony, and over all the vessels thereof and over all things that belong to it: they shall bear the tabernacle, and all the vessels thereof," and they shall minister unto it, and shall encamp round about the tabernacle " (vv.49-50).

As we will see, the census for the Levites would be taken separately--and based on a different criterion. So, they were "...not numbered among them "(v.47).

This was because the tribe of Levi was "set apart" and distinctive. It was detached from what was secular.

Dr. Michelle Corral

The remaining eleven tribes certainly had their own unique callings, but they were "earthly" and practical in nature, including engaging in warfare against the enemies of God. But the tribe of Levi was in a category all its own—consecrated by the Almighty for a sacred service.

CLASSIFICATION OF SEPARATION

The separation of the Levites speaks volumes to us today. I believe there are those who are reading these pages who have been called to walk in a special anointing. This will not come to fruition as you follow the rules and regulations of man or even try to live by a set of religious dictates and come under bondage. It is even futile to create certain rituals within yourself, thinking, "If I do this, I know the Lord will bless me."

This is not how God operates. We need to understand that to live with the anointing there is a consecration level and a detachment to the point where you are not like other believers. The Lord is not going to allow your actions and behavior to resemble other members in the church.

Instead, the Almighty is going to place you in a different spiritual classification. So what is lawful for another person to do, may not be lawful for you:

- ❖ A more powerful prayer life may be required.
- ❖ An elevated walk of love may be demanded.
- ❖ A greater life of sacrifice may be necessary.

Why? Because God has called you to be separated unto what is spiritual.

ATTENDANCE TO THE ANOINTING

The Levites experienced this distinct assignment from the Lord. Their call was to bear the burden of the tabernacle-- they were attendants to the anointing.

MC+

What we are discussing has absolutely nothing to do nothing do with our exterior.

Some people think being separated from the secular means you go around like a 'Holy Joe' or wear clothes which make you look as if you just walked out of a third-rate thrift store! Far from it. What we are discussing has absolutely nothing to do nothing do with our exterior. This concerns a deeper walk of the Spirit that transforms your mind, soul and spirit.

Not only were the Levites appointed to "minister" over the "Tent of Meeting" and all of its contents, they were told to "encamp round about the tabernacle" (Numbers 1:50).

In the literal sense of Scripture, this means they were divided from the rest and consecrated to such a degree that there was a physical distance between where they were encamped and where the other tribes pitched their tents in the wilderness. God told Moses, '...far off about the tabernacle of the congregation shall they pitch" (Numbers 2:2).

ATTENDANTS TO THE ANOINTING

If we could view this layout on a map, we would see how, during their wanderings, the tribes of Reuben, Asher, Ephraim and the others were distanced from the holy place, but the Levites remained close by----living in the very presence of God.

The other tribes were so removed they could only observe and visit the tabernacle.

Are you a prophetic Levite? Have you been called to be separated from the world and to be an attendant to the anointing?

MC+
Have you been called to be separated from the world and to be an attendant to the anointing?

I want to Be!

Dr. Michelle Corral

POSITIONED FOR POWER

There are wonderful, precious Christians who love the Lord and attend a house of worship on Sunday, but their calling is not to "look after" or be responsible for the anointing. However, if you are ready to move into a dimension where the Spirit of God literally envelops your life and you are willing to live in the atmosphere of heaven, the Lord will transform you into a spiritual Levite.

You will never come into the glory of the destiny God has prepared until you have been positioned in a place of power-and I believe the Lord has asked you to encamp around the tabernacle. He hasn't called you to what is secular, rather to what is sacred.

A HOVERING HEAVEN

If you have been chosen by God to be an attendant to the anointing, you will quickly realize if you are not near the presence of God it feels is if you are almost dying. Why? Because the Lord has ordained you as a spiritual Levite. You have been positioned to pitch your tent close to His glory.

What a marvelous place it is. Moses, and Aaron "looked toward the tabernacle of the congregation: and, behold, the cloud covered it, and the glory of the Lord appeared" (Numbers 16:42).

The tribe of Levi:

- ❖ Slept under the glory.
- ❖ Rose up in the morning under the glory.
- ❖ Served under the glory.
- ❖ Lived continually under the glory.

Scripture teaches that the Levite has been called to be perpetually in the Spirit's presence. When you move into this realm you hunger and thirst for the things of God--for worship, for praise. You just can't function unless He is with you.

PERPETUALLY IN HIS PRESENCE

I love the story in the Old Testament of Samuel when he was a little child. It is a parallel of how God will take a young Christian and call him to be a prophetic Levite and dwell constantly in the presence of the Lord.

When Samuel was only three years old, his mother, Hannah, took him to the temple and presented him to the Lord (1 Samuel 1:21-28).

As he grew, Samuel was not a priest even though he was a Levite-called to be an attendant to Eli, the high priest you to of Israel. Yet Samuel was chosen and destined to dwell in the presence of the Lord all the days of his life.

Again, we see how the atmosphere of heaven comes from being separated from what is secular. Where have you chosen to stake your tent? How close are you to the anointing of God?

SECOND:

WE HAVE ACCESS TO THE ANOINTING THROUGH SUBMISSION OF SELF IN THE SPIRIT

While not all Levites are priests, all priests are Levites.

How do we reconcile this statement? We need to understand there are four primary Levitical families. Three are attendants to the anointing-the sons of Gershon, Kohath and Merari (Numbers 3:17).

Then we have another family: Aaron and his sons who were exclusively priests. They were related to Kohath, but had a specific assignment.

The other families were responsible for the care of certain aspects of the tabernacle and only assisted the priests.

As we continue reading in Numbers, we find a separate census was about to take place. In the first national count, every male aged 20 and older was to be entered on the ledger. Why? Because they needed a record of those who were going to be in the armies of Israel and march to war.

It was a military census--and the Levites were excluded from this list because their battle was not the same as the rest of the tribes. Their warfare was spiritual--as the apostle Paul would one day write: "For the weapons of our warfare are not carnal, but mighty through God to the pulling down of strong holds" (2 Corinthians 10:4).

THE MANTLE AND MATURITY

Later, another census was taken-this time God told Moses and Aaron, "Take the sum of the sons of Kohath from among the sons of Levi, after their families, by the house of their fathers, from thirty years old and upward even until fifty years old, all that enter into the host, to do the work in the tabernacle of the congregation " (Numbers 4:2-3).

Why is a separate counting being called for this group? Because these were people who were involved in ministry, and the age of 30 is significant since it is a biblical reference to full maturity in Christ. When Jesus began His public ministry He was the exact same age-so we see a prophetic comparison between those who are going to bear the burden of the tabernacle.

You cannot carry the weight of such a responsibility if you

are spiritually childish and immature. It is necessary to be of "full age" to completely understand the call of God. There is a price to be paid for being an attendant to the anointing.

From my experience, the person who is still an infant the things of the Lord is consumed with self-interest. They constantly are thinking, How will this benefit me? What will it do for my life?

But the believer who reaches full age takes on the self personality of Jesus--someone who understands they have been ordained and sent by God and is dead to their own will and wants. Such an individual becomes a "servant of all " (Mark 9:35).

MC+
We have access to the anointing through total submission of self to the Spirit of God.

Again, we have access to the anointing through total submission of self to the Spirit of God.

BURDEN BEARERS OF GLORY

The sons of Kohath (related to Moses and Aaron) were told specifically what was required of them. They had a job description and a design for their destiny.

When the camp was to be relocated, they were in charge of the most holy things. For example, the Kohathites were to carry the Ark of the Covenant, the incense altar, lampstand (menorah), table of showbread and the sacred vessels-everything in the Holy of Holies.

This work was so divinely ordered that God told Moses and Aaron to go into the tabernacle and assign each man his task and what he was to carry, "But they shall not go in to see when the holy things are covered, lest they die" (Numbers 4:20).

This is in direct contrast to the two other Levitical families who were not to carry items from the inner sanctuary.

For example, the sons of Gershon were responsible for moving the curtains, the covering of the tabernacle, the draperies of the courtyard and the ropes and all the equipment (vv.25-36).

The sons of Merari were to transport "...the boards of the tabernacle, and the bars thereof... And the pillars of the court round about, and their sockets, and their pins, and their cords, With all their instruments, and With all their service " (vv.31-32).

By studying the rabbinic comments on these verses we learn the curtains carried by the sons of Gershon and the board moved by the sons of Merari did not have to be carried on poles, but rather on carts, driven by beasts of burden as directed by the Levites.

The only items carried on poles on the shoulders of the men of Kohath were taken from the Holy of Holies and the holy place.

GLORY TO GLORY!

The Bible is not dead history. Everything in God's Word has personal, powerful and prophetic relevance today.

> *MC+*
> *The word "covered" does not just mean wrapped. It refers to attending to the anointing and covering with glory.*

Moses gave instructions how everything in the inner sanctuary had to be "covered" with cloths of blue (Numbers 4:6-12).

The word "covered" does not just mean wrapped. It refers to attending to the anointing and covering with glory.

The choice of words in Scripture are not used at random. Moses concisely and precisely chose the word "covered" to compare with the wings of the cherubim-which covered the Ark (Exodus 25:20). God commanded Moses to drape the Ark with clothes of blue and badger skins (Numbers 4:6). This is prophetic prefiguring of how handling the power of His presence requires "covering."

The blue is symbolic of glory. In Exodus 24:10 the text teaches the glory is as a sapphire stone. The personal prophetic parallel is that when we cover with prayer and care, God's glory increases. This is what I call "attending to the anointing" --meaning you "cover" every aspect of life with prayer and care.

This also means when you "cover" your pastor the glory increases. And when you "cover" a work with a careful and prayerful attitude, again, the glory multiplies.

"SENSITIVITY" AND SURRENDER

There is a Hebrew concept called "snatching." It means to mishandle something sacred as though it were secular. It also refers to impulse rather than carefully calculating and comprehending while handling what is sacred.

In personal prophetic terms this refers to being surrendered surrender of and submitted to the Person and power of the Holy Spirit in all things. Yielding to Him requires "sensitivity" and surrender of one's self completely.

MC+

Yielding to Him requires "sensitivity" and surrender of one's self completely.

This is especially punctuated and accentuated when the presence of God is revealed in power.

DISCERNING THE DIFFERENCE

Remember, the concept of divine order is a primary principle in attaining access to the anointing.

In Scripture the sons of Kohath are itemized first because of their position of priority regarding the Ark of the Covenant.

Scripture also always itemizes the Ark of the Covenant first when defining the design of the tabernacle (Exodus 25). In modern terms, this places the priority of the presence of God over and above anything.

MC+

In order to access the atmosphere of heaven, the priority of His presence must be first and foremost in all things.

In order to access the atmosphere of heaven, the priority of His presence must be first and foremost in all things. This is a topic I frequently train and teach to my staff. On business days I handle God's work in detail with a meticulous manner. I want to be sure everything reflects excellence and perfection. I am a tough stickler for quality in His work.

However, on days when I preach and minister, my focus is diverted and different. I know I cannot mix what is secular with what is sacred. I will not even receive a phone call on ministry days unless it is an emergency.

I must surrender self to the Holy Spirit and I cannot allow my spirit to be distracted from hearing His voice. That's why I must spend time alone in prayer, surrendering my thoughts, my will and my entire being to the Holy Spirit.

MC+

I must spend time alone in prayer, surrendering my thoughts, my will and my entire being to the Holy Spirit.

I do this because I know if anyone sees Michelle Corral, I'm sunk! If they have their time alone eyes on me, they will miss the move of God. I must decrease so He can increase (John 3:30),

Please understand, beloved, I am not encouraging you to be "holier than thou." However, I want to teach you that when there is a great anointing, it is not business as usual.

Kathryn Kuhlman used to say that the night before the Shrine Auditorium meetings she barely slept one hour. She emphasized to us the continual importance of the responsibility of being surrendered completely to the Spirit.

We must make sure our priorities are in order. Where do we place our emphasis?

- ❖ Do we treat prayer as being in the inner sanctuary of God.
- ❖ Do we attend to the anointing?
- ❖ Do we assign a high value on being filled with the Holy Spirit?
- ❖ Do we place the healing power of God in the Holy of Holies?

SERVANTS OF THE SPIRIT

Beloved, I want you to understand we cannot access the anointing without submission to the Spirit. As spiritual Levites, we are called to bear the burdens of the things of God.

I also want you to understand this is not a burden like that of the carnal world. it is different in its nature. (Matthew 11:29). However, like the sons of Kohath from the tribe of Levi, you are carrying the weight of glory on your shoulders.

The sons of Kohath had to bear "down on their knees" in order to lift the weight of the Ark on their shoulders. This is a prophetic preview of every believer who is willing to be a servant of the Spirit.

In order to access the anointing, you willingly sacrifice time to be alone with God. This is how you bear down to carry the weight of glory on your knees.

MC+

In order to access the anointing, you willingly sacrifice time to be alone with God.

Beloved, if you desire a ministry that has the anointing to access the atmosphere of heaven to earth you must be a spiritual Levite and be willing to become humble for heaven's use.

We cannot consider the anointing like the poles and boards of the Tabernacle, which were carried on carts. The anointing must be accessed by placing the burden on a bar (like the Ark of the Covenant) and carried on our shoulders.

WAIT FOR THE WHISPER OF THE SPIRIT

Waiting for the Spirit's whisper means you've become so sensitive you can hear the slightest sound. As we will discuss in Chapter 6, when Elijah accessed a new anointing in his life (1 Kings 19:12) it was a whisper of the Spirit--a still small voice. This means his sensitivity

MC+

Waiting for the Spirit's whisper means you've become so sensitive you can hear the slightest sound.

increased to a new level.

This is the reason, as ministers, when we enter into His presence; we stay sensitive and surrendered to Him.

Beloved, my prayer is that you become so yielded that you follow everything as He prompts.

Father, I ask You to touch this
beloved one. Teach my dear friend how
to surrender self. Teach us Holy Spirit
how to wait for the Whisper of heaven.
Make us your spiritual Levites.

Dr. Michelle Corral

Chapter Three

Servants of the Service of God

Are you longing for the Lord to take you into a deeper walk in the Spirit? Do you hunger for a fresh encounter with the presence of God?

The secret is to become an attendant to the anointing – a servant of the service of God.

This is what Elisha was to the prophet Elijah. The Bible says he continually poured water on the hands of Elisha (2 Kings 3:11). He was *attending* to the anointing, enabling the prophet to enter into God's presence.

"Servants of the service" are those who are selected and elected to this important position. This is confirmed by the apostle Paul when he writes, *'Now be which stablisheth us with you in Christ, and hath anointed us, is God"* (2 Corinthians 1:21).

It is a continual touch of the Spirit which lives and abides in you. As Scripture declares, *"But the anointing which ye have received of him abideth in you, and ye need not that any man teach you: but as the same anointing teacheth you of all things, and is truth, and is no lie, and even as it hath taught you, ye shall abide in him"* (1 John 2:27).

It is clear that all Christians have been given a certain measure of anointing. *"But ye have an unction from the Holy One, and ye know all things "* (1 John 2:20). The word "unction" is synonymous with the anointing. And it is God's will that you understand you have been called and selected to care for what the Lord has placed upon you.

Otherwise, it is like an untended garden. Weeds will grow and choke what has been planted, and it will wither and die.

FOUR PROPHETIC PRINCIPLES

In the last chapter we saw how the tribe of Levi was set apart for the purpose of dealing with the spiritual matters of the children of Israel. Now I want to show you how it is possible for you to apply this knowledge and appropriate this revelation into your own life.

Regarding becoming servants of the service, there are four prophetic principles which can have a profound impact on your future:

PROPHETIC PRINCIPLE NUMBER ONE:
YOU HAVE BEEN PLEDGED FOR THE PRESENCE OF GOD

As we discussed, the Almighty gave Moses a directive to separate the tribe of Levi from the other eleven tribes of Israel. Their lives were pledged for the purpose of bringing God's presence to the earth.

The Bible says Moses and Aaron *"...shall offer the Levites before the Lord for an offering of the children of Israel, that they may execute the service of the Lord"* (Numbers 8:11).

MC+

God embraces the person who is separated in service and offered as a living sacrifice.

This God embraces the person who is separated in service and offered as a living sacrifice.

When you read in Scripture of the Levites, the Lord wants you to see *yourself*, called for the service of the anointing. There is a purpose for your existence: to carry with you--on your very being--the atmosphere of heaven and the presence of the

Spirit. The Lord is using you to help present His Spirit to this generation.

SATURATED BY THE SPIRIT

The life of the Levite had one specific objective: to minister unto the things of God. As Moses said, *"Bring the tribe of Levi near, and present them before Aaron the priest, that they may minister unto him"* (Numbers 3:6).

Remember, the Levites were actually divided into two major camps-the division of the priests (representing the anointing) and the division of the Levites (those who attended to the anointing).

The reason for ministering to the priests was so the selected servants who represented God's presence could flow with the anointing in Israel without interruption.

This is a unique assignment and those who are called to it have one common denominator: their purpose is to be of service to the individuals who do God's work on earth.

Speaking personally, our ministry is called "Breath of the Spirit" because it is our calling to bring the presence of the Spirit to God's people. Since the beginning, we have never changed our focus or vision.

A PROPHETIC PREVIEW

As a modern day Levite, your life is to be pledged for the presence of the Lord. As God told Moses, "...*the Levites shall be mine...*[and they shall] *go in to do the service of the tabernacle of the congregation...*[and you shall] *offer them for an offering"* (Numbers 8:14-15).

This was a prophetic preview of the calling of every believer who is anointed in Christ Jesus. Yes, you have been promised as an offering for the purpose of sharing the touch of the Spirit on earth.

MC+
You have been promised as an offering for the purpose of sharing the touch of the Spirit on earth.

The life of the Levite is paralleled in Paul's letter to the believers in Rome when he says, *"I beseech you therefore, brethren, by the mercies of God, that ye present your bodies a living sacrifice, holy, acceptable unto God, which is your reasonable service"* (Romans 12:1).

One woman told me, *"I thought I was doing God a favor when I was presenting my body as a living sacrifice."*

What she didn't understand was that it is only through the Holy Spirit--not through our works or our righteousness--that we are able to offer our body in such a way.

In its meaning, this is almost an identical text to the Lord telling Moses to *"...offer the Levites before the Lord for an offering of the children of Israel"* (Numbers 8:11).

The "Overcomers"

Your sacrificial service to the Lord is a pledge for the purpose of bringing the presence of God to earth.

I also want you to see this "offering" in light of what John wrote in the book of Revelation.

Much has been conjectured regarding the 144,000 who were sealed with the name of the Father on their foreheads (Revelation 7:3-4).

We need to see how this number is actually symmetric in the sense there are many symbols in Revelation which are tied prophetically with one another. For example, 12 is the number of the New Jerusalem--the redeemed bride of Christ--and appears throughout Revelation.

- ❖ There are 12 tribes of Israel (Revelation 7:5-8).
- ❖ There was a *"crown of twelve stars "* (Revelation 12:1).
- ❖ The holy city *"had a wall great and high, and had twelve gates, and at the gates twelve angels, and names written thereon: which are*

the names of the twelve tribes of the children of Israel" (Revelation 21:12).

❖ The wall of the city *"had twelve foundations, and in them the names of the twelve apostles of the Lamb"* (Revelation 21:14).

❖ The length, breadth and height of the city were equal--*"twelve thousand furlongs"* (Revelation 21:16).

❖ The city's *"twelve gates were twelve pearls"* (Revelation 21:21).

❖ In the midst of the city was *"the tree of life, which bare twelve manner of fruits, and yielded her fruit every month: and the leaves of the tree were for the healing of the nations"* (Revelation 22:2).

So when we see the 144,000, we need to realize it is <u>"not"</u> <u>in the context of "Rutherfordism"</u> or Jehovah Witness teaching. It is a misunderstanding of the text to conclude only 144,000 will be redeemed by Christ. This is symbolic and refers to those who have overcome.

YOU ARE SEALED BY THE SPIRIT

One of the major themes of Revelation is perseverance unto the end. The book itself begins with, *"I John, who also am your brother, and companion in tribulation, and in the kingdom and patience of Jesus Christ, was in the isle that is* called Patmos, for the word of God, and for the testimony of Jesus Christ" (Revelation 1:9).

John is not presenting himself as an apostle but is identifying with the church as one who is a "companion"--- one who suffered and was determined to endure.

What about those who were "sealed" with the name of the Father on their foreheads? This is also referenced in Scripture since we know as born again believers we are sealed with the Spirit of God: *"Now he which stablisheth us with you in Christ, and hath anointed us, is God; Who hath also sealed us, and given the earnest of the Spirit in our heart "* (2 Corinthians 1:22).

Revelation speaks of those who *"... were redeemed from among men, being the firstfruits unto God and to the Lamb"* (Revelation 14:4).

"Firstfruits" means their lives were an offering--they were living sacrifices redeemed among men.

MC+

"Lord, I am pledged for the purpose of Your presence."

Ask God to make you a present day Levite so you will be an offering unto the Lord for sacrificial service. Say, "Lord, I am pledged for the purpose of Your presence."

Dr. Michelle Corral

PROPHETIC PRINCIPLE NUMBER TWO:
YOU HAVE BEEN ELECTED FOR
AN EXISTENCE NOT OF THIS EARTH

Many don't understand their purpose and destiny. They are confused and discouraged, saying to themselves, "I don't seem to blend into what is going on." Or you might think, "Lord, I know what I should be doing, but I just can't seem to get it together."

Perhaps, just perhaps, God has a calling for your life, which is far above this human plane. He may have a heavenly purpose for you, which has yet to be revealed.

Remember, the Levites were elected for an existence not of this earth--so much so they weren't even included in the national numbers.

Jesus is speaking of believers when He declares, *"They are not of the world, even as I am not of it"* (John 17:16).

You have been chosen for a higher calling. As the apostle Paul says, *"But God forbid that I should glory, save in the cross of our Lord Jesus Christ, by whom the world is crucified unto me, and I unto the world"* (Galatians 6:14).

"CHOSEN OF THE CHOSEN"

It is perfectly understandable that those who live in the flesh cannot relate to one who is set apart unto the Lord for service: *"Behold, what manner of love the Father hath bestowed upon us, that we should be called the sons of God: therefore the world knoweth us not, because it knew him not"* (1 John 3:1).

The Bible tells us, *"friendship of the world is enmity with God"* (James 4:4). So when we see the Levites segregated in the national numbering, God is clarifying this important principle: He separates His chosen vessels.

The whole nation of Israel was called, yet only the tribe of Levi was chosen. This foreshadows how Jesus Christ teaches us that we are in the world, but not of the world.

MC+
Are you willing to walk in the Spirit and be the "chosen of the chosen?"

Are you willing to walk in the Spirit and be the "chosen of the chosen?"

The Almighty spoke to Moses to prepare the people so the power of God would fall on them. Until Israel was in complete divine order, the clouds of glory could not come in their fullness.

Dr. Michelle Corral

Every tribe knew exactly where they were to be located, and it was their position which brought them power.

Many believers today do not fully comprehend their position in Christ. As a result, the entire church grows weak and feeble. However, as each of us fulfill our calling, the power of the Spirit begins to move supernaturally.

PREDESTINED FOR PURPOSE

In the last chapter we spoke of a national census where those 20 and up were numbered, and a special Levitical census counting those 30 and above (representing spiritual maturity in those who were anointed).

Now let me tell you about one additional census taken among the Levites. God told Moses: *"Number the children of Levi after the house of their fathers, by their families: every male from a month old and upward"* (Numbers 3:15).

There's a big difference between a census which began at age 20 (for 11 tribes) and one which counted those starting from one month of birth (for the Levites).

Why did the Lord order this? The Scripture is prophetically symbolizing how God positions you for purpose even prior to your birth. As the Almighty told the prophet Jeremiah, *"Before I formed thee in the belly I knew thee; and before thou camest forth out of the womb I sanctified thee, and I ordained thee a prophet unto the nations"* (Jeremiah 1:5).

The Lord was telling the Levites---and is saying to you---"From your beginning, I have chosen you to be Mine. Everything about you has a design toward destiny."

SELECTED AND ELECTED

Scripture clarifies between coincidence and providence.

Coincidence says, "Oh, those things just happened. But providence says, "No, although you have made mistakes, I'm turning them into miracles!"

Regardless of what may have occurred in your childhood--including being used or abused--God is assuring you, "I am going to use your life for My honor and glory."

You can claim the promise of the Word: *"And we know that all things work together for good to them that love God, to them who are the called according to his purpose"* (Romans 8:28).

Praise God! We have been elected for an existence not of this earth.

PROPHETIC PRINCIPLE NUMBER THREE:
YOU ARE SELECTED TO LIVE PERPETUALLY IN GOD'S PRESENCE

Most people have no concept of how powerful the anointing of the Lord was in the tabernacle of the children of Israel during their journey toward the Promised Land.

Oh, we read of the "glory cloud," yet it was more than a visual symbol hovering over the Tent of Meeting. The presence of God was inside, outside, on top of and completely surrounding this holy place.

Here's what Scripture records: *"Then a cloud covered the tent of the congregation, and the glory of the Lord filled the tabernacle. And Moses was not able to enter into the tent of the congregation, because the cloud abode thereon, and the glory of the Lord filled the tabernacle"* (Exodus 40:34-35).

Can you imagine an anointing so awesome you couldn't even walk into the sanctuary? That's the atmosphere in which Moses and the Levites lived.

MC+

Can you imagine an anointing so awesome you couldn't even walk into the sanctuary?

49

The Bible tells us the cloud was so strong it appeared as a fire over the tabernacle all night long (Numbers 9:15-16).

AN ABIDING ANOINTING

God is telling you this moment to stay close to the presence of His Spirit. If the anointing is on you, remain right where you are. And if you see it moving, follow where the Spirit leads. This is exactly what the tribes of Israel did.

Led by Moses, "...*as long as the cloud abode upon the tabernacle they rested in their tents... [And] whether it were two days, or a month, or a year, that the cloud tarried upon the tabernacle, remaining thereon, the children of Israel abode in their tents, and journeyed not: but when it was taken up, they journeyed"* (Numbers 9:18,22).

This is how the Levites remained perpetually in God's presence.

Does this mean the other eleven tribes were not blessed by the Lord or experienced His miracles in the wilderness? No. We know for a fact that all the tribes:

- ❖ Were delivered from the attacking Egyptians by God parting the Red sea (Exodus 14:21-23).
- ❖ Were nourished when the bitter waters of Marah were made sweet (Exodus 15:25).

- ❖ Were fed with manna that dropped from heaven (Exodus 16:13-36).
- ❖ Drank from water, which suddenly gushed out of a rock (Exodus 17:58).

Every tribe from Asher to Zebulun enjoyed God's favor, yet the Levites were particularly blessed and they were called to live continually in His presence.

THE COVERING OF THE CLOUD

I am praying that the Almighty will call you to live under the glory cloud. When He does, you will walk any distance and pay any price to stay where His Spirit dwells. As David pleaded, *"Cast me not away from thy presence; and take not thy holy spirit from me"* (Psalm 51:11).

MC+

I am praying that the Almighty will call you to live under the glory cloud.

The psalmist also stated, *"One thing have I desired of the Lord, that will I seek after; that I may dwell in the house of the Lord all the days of my life, to behold the behold of Lord, and to inquire in his temple"* Psalm 27:4)

Does this mean we should set up physical residence in the sanctuary of the Lord? Of course not. David didn't camp out in the tabernacle, but he did live under an invisible covering of God's Spirit day and night.

Dr. Michelle Corral

The Lord's "covering" continually followed David, and he couldn't exist without the anointing.

PROPHETIC PRINCIPLE NUMBER FOUR:
YOU ARE CHOSEN TO LABOR
IN THE HOUSE OF THE LORD

The Levites were brought before the entire assembly of the children of Israel and presented as an offering of sacrifice to the Lord. Their assignment was to work in the sanctuary of God.

Scripture tells that under the direction of the priest (Aaron), *"... they shall keep his charge...to do the service [the physical labor] of the tabernacle"* (Numbers 3:7).

This was confirmed by the laying on of hands. God told Moses to *"...bring the Levites before the Lord and the children of Israel shall put their hands upon the Levites: And Aaron shall offer the Levites before the Lord for an offering of the children of Israel, that they may execute the service [the work] of the Lord"* (Numbers 8:10-11).

In the New Testament, the laying on of hands speaks to the impartation of God's anointing. In this instance, however, it was a visual act of the people "leaning" on, or reaching out, to the Levites because they represented the sacrifice-- the offering.

In those days, when an offering was brought to the priest he would literally press his hand on the head of what was presented. The concept is one of transferring strength on what is being sacrificed.

So, when the Scripture says, *"Israel shall put their hands upon the Levites,"* it meant the entire nation was going to place their strength onto this tribe and would serve as a pledge to bring the presence of God to Israel and keep the power of God flowing.

MC+

The entire nation was going to place their strength onto this tribe.

THE TOIL OF THE TABERNACLE

These are prophetic symbols of those who have the anointing and have been called to labor and bear the burden of the spiritual sanctuary.

The life of the Levite was to toil for the tabernacle (Numbers 1:50). *"And when the tabernacle setteth forward the Levites shall take it down: and when the tabernacle is to be pitched, the Levites shall set it up* (v.51).

When the Bible says the Levites "pitched" the tabernacle, the word in Hebrew means "raised up." This also tells us they didn't just physically raise up the tabernacle, but they lifted up the anointing to it's highest level.

MC+
Everything pertaining to the tabernacle was planned and designed to be of the highest standard.

Everything pertaining to the tabernacle was planned and designed to be of the highest standard. The finest craftsmen worked with gold, silver, bronze, wood, cloth and precious jewels to create the elements of the tabernacle exactly as God directed Moses (Exodus 25-31).

When it was completed, the Almighty said: *'And thou shalt take the anointing oil, and anoint the tabernacle, and all that is therein, and shalt hallow it, and all the vessels thereof: and it shall be holy"* (Exodus 40:9).

BEARING YOUR BURDEN ON A BAR

Today, as His prophetic Levites, we are bearing the burden of the glory of God. We must be willing to toil for the tabernacle.

Access to the anointing requires we incorporate the concept of the Levite. They didn't half-way construct the sanctuary where God was to be worshiped, but they made sure it was fully and perfectly assembled. Even more, this was a labor of love and an effort of excellence.

Today, we are carrying the Ark of the Covenant on our shoulders. Like the sons of Kohath, we are bearing the burden on a bar. We don't know what it looks like, yet we feel its weight. And even though it is covered, we are familiar with the presence of God and sense the things of heaven through the Spirit.

You don't have to visibly see the anointing to know it is real. In the days of the Levites, only the high priest could look at what was in the Holy of Holies. The other members of the tribe "...shall not go in to see when the holy things are covered, lest they die" (Numbers 4:20).

GIFTS OF GRACE

As I write these words, I pray you are hungry to understand the anointing in a greater way. As Paul writes, *"Now concerning spiritual gifts, brethren, I would not have you ignorant"* (1 Corinthians 12:1).

It is God's will for you to receive all He has for you. That's why you are to *"...desire spiritual gifts"* (1 Corinthians 14:1).

While we are to earnestly seek for the best gifts, Paul says, *"...yet show I unto you a more excellent way"* (1 Corinthians 12:31). He did not disparage the work of the Spirit, rather he was encouraging believers to emulate excellence in ministry. This is perfectly and prophetically prefigured through the Levites.

Remember:

- ❖ You have been pledged for the presence of God.
- ❖ You have been elected for an existence not of this earth.
- ❖ You are selected to live perpetually in God's presence.
- ❖ You are chosen to labor in the house of the Lord.

With thanksgiving in your heart raise your hands to heaven and shout, "I am a servant of the service of God."

Chapter Four

The Empoweing Effects of The Anointing

One of the most powerful stories in the Hebrew Scriptures is how Jacob gave his son, Joseph, the coat of many colors.

As we will see, this was much more than a father presenting a gift to a son. The coat represents the empowering effects of God's anointing--and is a garment your Heavenly Father longs to place on you today.

Scripture tells us, "Now Israel loved Joseph more than all his children, because he was the son of his old age: and he made him a coat of many colors" (Genesis 37:3). "Israel" is the spiritual name God gave Jacob.

If you read the story in its entirety, you know that Joseph was not the firstborn. Yet, of Jacob's twelve sons, Joseph was loved above all the rest? Why was this true? Let's look at the genealogy.

The Bible declares, "These are the generations of Jacob. Joseph, being seventeen years old..." (v.2).

We know from the record there were several sons born to Jacob prior to this, yet this verse documents that Joseph is classified and categorized as the heir to the Abrahamic covenant.

The genealogy actually skips ten of Jacob's sons--from Reuben to Zebulun--and goes directly to Joseph. It is the first time anything like this is presented in Scripture.

THE CONFERRING OF THE COAT

In the New Testament, the first chapter of the gospel of Matthew records a genealogy, which traces the lineage of Jesus from the House of David. However, from the patriarchs to David there are several generations not listed. But the reason for their exclusion is for brevity--not because God eliminated them from the bloodline.

In Joseph's case it was different. You see, the Almighty removed the birthright from Jacob's firstborn, Reuben. The coat we read about became a conferred covenant of blessing on the life of Joseph.

In those days, the first born automatically received all the benefits of birthright--including being an heir to the greatest portion of the father's estate. There is indication if there was a major transgression, such an honor could be transferred to another son. This is what happened in the case of Reuben. He committed an immoral sexual act by sleeping with Bilhah, the handmaid of his step-mother Rachel (Genesis 35:22).

The Bible records, "Now the sons of Reuben the firstborn of Israel...for he was the firstborn; but, forasmuch as he defiled his father's bed, his birthright was given unto the sons Joseph the son of Israel: and the genealogy is not to be reckoned after the birthright"(1 Chronicles 5:1).

So, instead of the birthright remaining with the firstborn son of Leah, it is now bestowed on the firstborn son of Rachel.

This demonstrates that if we are not faithful to His commands we can lose what is rightfully ours. That's why the Bible counsels us to, "Remember therefore how thou hast received and heard,

MC+

If we are not faithful to His commands we can lose what is rightfully ours.

and hold hast..." (Revelation 3:3).

THE PEDIGREE OF PRIESTHOOD

In the literal context of the story, we see the rights conferred on Joseph as a pedigree of priesthood in his family.

The coat of many colors represented far more than a mere garment. It expressed the bestowing of the anointing on a chosen vessel.

It's important to understand that even though we read of the priesthood resting on Aaron and his sons, it wasn't always present in this manner. During the time of the patriarchs, the firstborn son of every house was the priest of the home. After the children of Israel came out of Egypt, God spoke to Moses and said, "Sanctify unto me all the firstborn, whatsoever openeth the womb among the children of Israel...it is mine" (Exodus 13:1-2).

This meant the first son could not be involved in secular activity--they were the spiritual leaders of the household.

However, this was not a permanent, guaranteed lifelong designation. If the firstborn son committed a grievous error--as in the case of Reuben--a man could lose his birthright. It is also why we need to be "stedfast, unmoveable, always abounding in the work of the Lord, forasmuch as ye know that your labour is not in vain in the Lord" (1 Corinthians 15:58).

FULFILLMENT BY WHAT WAS FORFEITED

During their wandering in the wilderness, there was a time when the children of Israel rebelled and bowed before a golden calf (Exodus 32). This caused righteous anger to rise within Moses. He stood at the gate of the camp and asked, "Who is on the Lord's side? let him come unto me. And all the sons of Levi gathered themselves together unto him" (Exodus 32:26).

It was one more reason the Lord anointed and consecrated the Levites for service. Now, instead of the firstborn being the priest of the family, this designation was given to the Levites.

By worshiping false gods, the oldest sons of the children of Israel forfeited their birthright.

By worshiping false gods, the oldest sons of the children of Israel forfeited their birthright--as did Reuben.

ESAU, THE DESTINY DESPISER

Joseph's own father, Jacob, was not a firstborn, yet he was the recipient of the anointing. Isaac and Rebekah had twin sons, Jacob and Esau--but Esau was born first.

One day, when the sons were older, Jacob was preparing a pot of lentil stew for his dying father when Esau returned from hunting. He was famished and said to his brother, "Feed me, I pray thee, with that same red pottage; for I am faint...And Jacob said, Sell me this day thy birthright" (Genesis 25:30-31).

Think of it! Esau thought so little of his birthright he sold it for a simple pot of beans! "Then Jacob gave Esau bread and pottage of lentiles; and he did eat and drink, and rose up, and went his way: thus Esau despised his birthright" (v.34).

Even more, as Isaac wanted one last meal and while Esau was out searching for it, Rebekah saw the chance for Isaac to give his blessing to her beloved son Jacob. So she "...took goodly raiment of her eldest son Esau, which were with her in the house, and put them upon Jacob her younger son" (Genesis 27:15).

MC+

The "godly raiment" was the coat—the pedigree of priesthood.

The "godly raiment" was the coat-- the pedigree of priesthood.

This is what Esau should have been wearing when he went game hunting--and he also should have sacrificed to the Lord an offering that he caught. But his birthright was of no consequence to him and the coat was left hanging in the closet.

Dr. Michelle Corral

Bestowing the Blessing

As Jacob approached his father in this "godly raiment," the Bible records what Isaac said: "Come near now, and kiss me, my son. And he came near, and kissed him: and he smelled the smell of his raiment, and blessed him, and said, See, the smell of my son is as the smell of a field which the Lord hath blessed: Therefore God give thee of the dew of heaven, and the fatness of the earth, and plenty of corn and wine: Let people serve thee, and nations bow down to thee: be lord over thy brethren, and let thy mother's sons bow down to thee: cursed be every one that curseth thee, and blessed be he that blesseth thee" (VV.26-29).

Not only did Jacob have the birthright, he also now received the blessing of Isaac.

This was a prelude to Jacob, himself, bestowing the robe of anointing on his own son, Joseph.

Garments of Glory

You see, when the priesthood was established, the garments were anointed. For example, in Exodus we read how God told Moses, "take thou unto thee Aaron thy brother; and his sons with him, from among the children of Israel, that he may minister unto me in the priest's office...and thou shalt make holy garments for Aaron thy brother for glory and for beauty. And thou shalt speak unto all that are wise hearted, whom I have filled with the spirit of wisdom, that they may make Aaron's garments to consecrate him, that he may minister unto me in the priest's office " (Exodus 28:l-3).

Later in the same chapter we learn: "And thou shalt embroider the coat of fine linen... And for Aaron's sons thou shalt make coats...And thou shalt put them upon Aaron thy brother, and his sons with him; and shalt anoint them, and consecrate them, and sanctify them, that they may minister unto me" (vv.39-41).

This is a powerful lesson. Aaron and his sons could not function in the priestly ministry or destiny the Father had for them without the coat--representing the very presence of God.

The anointing, "...is like the precious ointment upon the head, that ran down upon the beard, even Aaron's beard: that went down to the skirts of his garments" (Psalm 133:2).

PARTICIPATION IN PRIESTHOOD

So many Christians leave their coat hanging in the closet. They have not understood what the Lord has promised-- what their Heavenly Father conferred on them as a birthright and a blessing through the anointing.

Dr. Michelle Corral

The Lord is calling you to a priesthood not of the flesh, but of the Spirit.

Even now, your prayer should be, "Lord, I am ready to receive the coat. I want to worship You with the anointing on my life."

God has a royal robe He desires to place over your shoulders. It is the Father's way of bestowing your spiritual birthright and His blessing.

MC+

Don't be an Esau and leave your garment in the closet! Wear it with joy and give God the glory.

Don't be an Esau and leave your garment in the closet!

As we prophetically parallel this amazing coat of many colors, we will find three empowering effects of the anointing on your personal life.

THE FIRST EMPOWERING EFFECT OF THE ANOINTING:
YOU WILL PARTICIPATE IN WHAT IS PROPHETIC

Prior to the coat of many colors being placed on Joseph, we have no record that he was a dreamer. But when the anointing touched the life of this young man, his mind began to overflow with destiny dreams. They were not only significant, they were supernatural.

What Joseph dreamed concerning the future, was absolutely inconceivable--and it involved his brothers. You can imagine the envy and jealousy which already existed because Jacob showed such love toward Joseph, especially when he was given the multi-colored coat.

Now Joseph asked his brothers to gather around and he said, "Hear, I pray you, this dream which I have dreamed: For, behold, we were binding sheaves in the field, and, lo, my sheaf arose, and also stood upright; and, behold, your sheaves stood round about, and made obeisance to my sheaf. And his brethren said to him, Shalt thou indeed reign over us? or shalt thou indeed have dominion over us? And they hated him yet the more for his dreams, and for his words" (Genesis 37:6-8).

Then Joseph had another dream which he shared with not only his brothers, but also his father. This time he saw the sun, moon and eleven stars bowing down to him. (v.9).

Jacob asked, "What is this dream that thou hast dreamed? Shall I and thy mother and thy brethren indeed come to bow down ourselves to thee to the earth?" (v.10)

The brothers were once again indignant, yet Jacob pondered the dream in his heart.

DREAMS AND DESTINY

Who could have known these dreams foretold that Joseph would one day rule Egypt with Pharaoh's blessing and the famine-starved people in Canaan--including Joseph's own family--would come and humble themselves before him asking for food?

You don't enter into God's greatness as a result of your own power, strength, talent, will, ability or through your connections. No, when the presence of the Lord is on your life, you come into your destiny only because of the anointing.

MC+

When the presence of the Lord is on your life, you come into your destiny only because of the anointing.

Scripture is clear that once the coat was conferred on Joseph, he rose to power in Egypt as a direct result of participating in what was prophetic. He not only dreamed dreams, but God gave him the ability to interpret them.

FORETELLING FAMINE

One night, Pharaoh had a dream that involved him standing on the bank of the Nile. Seven well nourished cows come out of the river, followed by seven scrawny cows--and the seven ugly cows ate up the seven healthy ones. The same scenario was repeated with seven heads of grain on a good stalk being eaten up by seven thin, scorched heads of grain.

Pharaoh called for all the wise men and magicians of Egypt, but they failed to interpret the dream.

Finally, his butler remembered being in prison with Joseph two years earlier and told Pharaoh about "...a young man, an Hebrew, servant to the captain of the guard; and we told him, and be interpreted to us our dreams" (Genesis 41:12).

Immediately, Pharaoh had Joseph brought to him from the prison, and when the dream was repeated once more, Joseph offered this interpretation. There would be seven years of great abundance in Egypt followed by seven years of devastating famine.

SATURATED BY THE SPIRIT

The king decided to prepare for the impending scarcity by finding someone who could prepare for such an eventuality and store up the grain. He asked his servants, "Can we find such a one as this is, a man in whom the Spirit of God is?" (v.38).

No sooner had Pharaoh uttered those words when he turned to Joseph and announced, "Forasmuch as God hath showed thee all this, there is none so discreet and wise as thou art: Thou shalt be over my house, and according unto thy word shall all my people be ruled: only in the throne will I be greater than thou. And Pharaoh said unto Joseph, See, I have set thee over all the land Egypt" (vv.39-41).

Even Pharaoh, who did not know the Lord, recognized the "Spirit of God" was on this man--and Joseph was positioned to the place of his anointing. Once more, a robe would be draped around his shoulders and the dream he had at the age of seventeen was now being fulfilled.

Remember, Joseph could not have been a dreamer without the coat--a symbol of the Spirit of God.

Don't ever be afraid of receiving the garment of the anointing. It will allow you to participate in what is prophetic.

MC+

Joseph could not have been a dreamer without the coat – a symbol of the Spirit of God.

THE SECOND EMPOWERING
EFFECT OF THE ANOINTING:
YOU WILL BE COMMISSIONED FOR A MISSION

MC+

When the coat of the anointing is placed over your life you will receive your marching orders from on high.

When the coat of the anointing is placed over your life you will receive your marching orders from on high. We mentioned this briefly in the first chapter, but now I want you to see how it empowers and prepares you for action.

The anointing is not the objective, it is the means to accomplish God's plan and purpose for you. Here's how the prophet Isaiah expresses this principle: "The spirit of the Lord God is upon me; because the Lord hath anointed me to preach good tidings unto the meek; he hath sent me to bind up the brokenhearted, to proclaim liberty to the captives, and the opening of the prison to them that are bound" (Isaiah 61:1).

What is the purpose? To preach, to send, to proclaim and to liberate.

SAY "YES"

The Lord may not ask you to be a missionary and travel to the ends of the earth, but He has a specific ministry assignment just for you. Instead, He could call you to work with teens or be an intercessor in prayer.

We see this power principle operating in the history of Joseph because when the coat was conferred on him, then God gave him a mission.

The Lord didn't announce "You are going to be the ruler of Egypt"--that would be many years down the road. Instead, God whispered in his ear, "I want you to say 'Yes.' Do whatever I tell you."

Here was Joseph's first assignment. Jacob said to his son, "Do not thy brethren feed the flock in Shechem? come, and I will send thee unto them" (Genesis 37:12).

Joseph, realizing how much his brothers hated him, could have loudly protested. But he was anointed and gave this obedient reply: "Here am I" (v.12).

A casual observer would say this was the worst day of Joseph's life-considering he never returned to his father's house. However, it turned out to be a day of destiny.

It is difficult to understand how much his brothers despised Joseph. Because their father favored him, "...they hated him, and could not speak peaceably unto him" (v.4). And every time he shared one of his dreams, "...they hated him yet the more"(v.8).

Yet, because of God's covering, Joseph was able to be with his siblings who persecuted him.

These texts prophetically prefigure how we are commissioned with a mission. Like Joseph, the anointing will take you to a place of death and destiny.

"GOD'S BREAD PROVIDER"

His father sent him on a mission to meet his brothers in Shechem. In reality, Jacob was (without knowing it) commissioning his son to be a slave in Egypt--and for the next 22 years would not see his face. Joseph spent 13 of those years languishing in the house of Potipher and the prison. But behind it all was God's purpose.

Sold into slavery by his own brothers for 20 pieces of silver (Genesis 27:28), Joseph rose to become second in command to only Pharaoh and eventually saved his people from famine as "God's bread provider."

In preserving this marvelous story, the Lord wants us to understand how Joseph had a willing heart--and would have said "Here am I" even if he knew the intimate details of the struggle ahead. His life prefigures the process of loss for the cross of Jesus. Joseph's brothers finally journeyed from Canaan to seek bread in Egypt for their starving people. Of course, they had to bow before Joseph, not knowing who this noble governor truly was. This also fulfilled the dream God had given more than two decades earlier.

PAIN USED FOR PURPOSE

After Joseph's identity was revealed, the brothers were terrified, fearing retribution for trying to take his life, throwing him in a pit and eventually selling him to a band of Ishmaelites.

But, because of the anointing, Joseph viewed things from a heavenly perspective. He saw his pain used toward the purpose of God. That's why he was able to say, "...be not grieved, nor angry with yourselves, that ye sold me hither: for God did send me before you to preserve life" (Genesis 45:5).

MC+

Because of the anointing, Joseph viewed things from a heavenly perspective.

He was telling them, "I was commissioned with a mission. When the coat was placed on me, God had a destiny in mind. When my father sent me that day and you sold me to those Ishmaelites to be taken down into Egypt, the Lord already had a destiny for the darkest days of my life."

He assured his brothers, "...God sent me before you to preserve you a posterity in the earth, and to save your lives by a great deliverance" (v. 7).

FAITH BY FIRE

Moses, as the author of Genesis, certainly could identify with Joseph saying "Here am I."

Earlier, in Genesis 22, we find the story of Abraham facing his greatest test of faith. The Lord was about to ask him to offer his son, Isaac, on the altar of sacrifice. What was Abraham's answer when God called him? This man, in whom the Lord promised the nations of the world would be blessed, replied, "Behold, here I am" (Genesis 22:22).

Joseph and Abraham represent the "Here am I" believers who are willing to pick up their cross and follow the Lord--a readiness to fulfill His Great Commission and mission for the sake of Christ and the gospel.

Dr. Michelle Corral

The Third Empowering
Effect of the Anointing:
Finding Favor with Your Father

Because we tend to interpret Scripture from a carnal context, we have a difficult time trying to understand Why Jacob loved Joseph so much.

To help us see things from God's perspective, the Lord uses the name "Israel"--the spiritual designation for Jacob. The verse reads: "Now Israel loved [Joseph more than all his children..."(Genesis 37:3).

Is God blessing favoritism? Not at all. What the Scripture is communicating is that there was a certain element of divine favor on Joseph because the coat was conferred on his life.

As we discover, Joseph not only found favor with his earthly father, he had the blessing and favor of his Heavenly Father because of the anointing.

Even in the midst of confusion in a foreign land, and not sure what the Almighty was doing in his circumstance, Scripture records, "And the Lord was with Joseph, and be was a prosperous man; and he was in the house of his master the Egyptian" (Genesis 39:2). Yes, the Lord was with him and showed Joseph mercy--and gave him favor in the sight of the keeper of the prison.

MC+

When the anointing arrives you will find favor.

It doesn't matter what kind of pain you are traveling through, when the anointing arrives you will find favor. Most important, you personally know the King of Kings who can cause everything to change. Only He can miraculously lift you from a treacherous pit to a prosperous place.

The result of being immersed in the anointing is a connecting component throughout Scripture. I'm not talking about a small touch from heaven, rather an overwhelming blessing to the person who pursues the "coat" regardless of the pain, or the loss for the cross of Jesus.

FINDING FAVOR WITH THE KING

I love the story of Esther. She didn't stand out in the crowd just because she was pretty. Certainly, she was, "fair and beautiful" (Esther 2:7), but there were scores of such women in the harem of King Ahasuerus.

But why did he love Esther above all the others? The answer is prophetically paralleled to the reason Jacob loved Joseph more than his other sons. There is something about the anointing which brings divine favor on an individual's life.

In Esther's case, "Now when every maid's turn was come to go in to king Ahasuerus, after that she had been twelve months, according to the manner of the women, (for so were the days of their purifications accomplished to wit, six months with oil of myrrh, and six months with sweet odours, and with other things for the purifying of the women;) " (Esther 2:12).

Every candidate for queen went through the same purification process, but "...Esther obtained favour in the sight of all them that looked upon her"(v,15). And the Bible tells us, "...the king loved Esther above all the women, and she obtained grace and favour in his sight more than all the virgins; so that he set the royal crown upon her head, and made her queen" (v.17).

The context conveys God caused Esther to be loved by the king and find favor for such a position because there was an anointing and purpose on her life. If you read the entire story you discover she was sent "for such a time as this" (Esther 4:14) to save her people from utter destruction.

CHRIST-LIKE CHARACTER

The anointing is not something you occasionally feel or casually experience. It is the presence of God which rests upon you--and is your most precious possession.

Remember, if you have the anointing you will automatically begin to participate in what is prophetic. The Lord will give you revelation. You may not dream dreams on your pillow, but you are going to have a vision in your heart which will direct you into destiny.

As God places the anointed "coat" on your life, He will love you in His own unique way. The anointing makes you become more like Jesus. It produces the power of Christ-like character.

You have already received the righteousness of God in Christ, yet the reason the Father wants you to have access to the anointing is so you will be persistent in pursuing a Christ-like character--to see the way He sees, talk the way He talks and walk the way He walks.

The Father also desires to say about you, "I see Jesus in my child, in whom I am well pleased." You will find favor with Him.

A DESTINY DECISION

Perhaps the Lord is dealing with you concerning decisions that have detoured your destiny. Maybe you did not realize you sold your birthright for something trivial. Or, it could be your coat of anointing has been left abandoned in a closet and it's time to ask the Lord to let you wear it once more.

At one point you may have had a close relationship with the Holy Spirit and have had a passion to please Him. Beloved, you can have that relationship restored.

When the blood of Jesus is applied to every area of your life, the spirit of death cannot enter.

Please don't remove the garment of the anointing.

Just before Aaron died, God told Moses to go up into the mountain, "And strip Aaron of his garments" (Numbers 20:26). And he died there.

Although Aaron was chronologically advanced in years, perhaps his days could have continued if the coat had not been removed. I believe this is a message for us right now. This prefigures prophetically how the coat confers life through the anointing.

Dr. Michelle Corral

When the coat of anointing is configured on you, death or destruction cannot touch your family. I'm not referring to physical death, rather bondage and blocks that chain and restrain you.

Now is the time to restore God's power and presence. Welcome and embrace His Spirit and robe yourself in His righteousness. You will experience the empowering effects of the anointing.

Chapter Five

The Samuel Secret

In the days before Samuel came to his prophetic office, there was utter chaos rampant in Israel. For 40 years the Philistines had run roughshod throughout the land.

Scripture records the extent of Israel's military blundering. In one battle, "...the Philistines put themselves in array against Israel: and when they joined battle, Israel was smitten before the Philistines: and they slew of the army in the field about four thousand men"(1 Samuel 4:2).

It is obvious that in the natural Israel did not have the might or strength to subdue their arch enemy--and even the Ark of the Covenant was captured. The "...Philistines fought, and Israel was smitten, and they fled every man into his tent: and there was a very great slaughter; for there fell of Israel thirty thousand footmen. And the ark of God was taken; and the two sons of Eli, Hophni and Phinehas, were slain"(vv. 10-11).

The reason these defeats were significant is because it is symbolic. God was about to turn the situation around--not through the power of the Israeli army or military might, but by an anointing which rested on one of God's prophets, Samuel.

This prophet propelled his generation to a place of power. This is a prophetic prefiguring to an apostolic anointing poured upon the church today. Samuel prefigures the power that is both priestly and prophetic.

APOSTOLIC AUTHORITY

If territory is taken because of the attacks of Satan, when the anointing is present, everything will be restored-your health, strength, marriage, ministry, gifts of the Spirit and the unmistakable power of God on your life. I believe the "alabaster box" containing the ointment of heaven is about to be broken over you (Luke 7:37-38).

When Samuel was positioned in his prophetic office, strongholds were broken: the "...Philistines were subdued, and they came no more into the coast of Israel: and the hand of the Lord was against the Phillistines all the days of Samuel" (1 Samuel 7:13).

There is an amazing authority in the anointing that subdues strongholds, principalities and powers. As the apostolic anointing increases, there will be a restoration in the ruins of taken territory. "And he gave me some, apostles; and some, prophets; and some, evangelists; and some, pastors and teachers" (Ephesians 4:11).

It is time we pray to the Spirit of God and ask Him to place in position those He has ordained in areas of apostolic authority.

A DIVINE DESIGN

Remember, all the strength of the Israeli army could not subdue the forces of the Philistines until Samuel took his prophetic office. This is important because there is a divine design in the body of Christ which is connected to the future of every believer.

MC+

All the strength of the Israeli army could not subdue the forces of the Philistines until Samuel took his prophetic office.

My destiny is connected to your destiny and we are joined in this battle together: "For we wrestle not against flesh and blood, but against principalities, against powers, against the rulers of the darkness of this world, against spiritual wickedness in high places" (Ephesians 6:12). "For though we walk in the flesh, we do not war after the flesh: (For the weapons of our warfare are not carnal, but mighty through God to the pulling down of strong holds;)" (2 Corinthians 10:3-4).

As we will learn, beloved, the "Samuel Secret" subdues strongholds and positions you for power over the wiles of the wicked one.

There are five "power principles" involved:

THE FIRST POWER PRINCIPLE:

TAKE BACK THE TERRITORY

God had you in mind when the Bible was written--and there is a prophetic word for you personally in every portion of Scripture.

MC+

God has you in mind when the Bible was written.

Subduing the strongholds of Israel corresponds to the Lord's deliverance and destiny in your life. Of course, our human nature would like to see things restored overnight, but the Almighty has His own timetable. In the case of Israel, victory over the Philistines took four long decades. In fact, the hold was so strong it required more than one deliverer.

The first person destined to deliver Israel out of the hand of the Philistines was Samson. He was called by the Lord for a design of destiny.

Scripture tells us how an angel came to a barren woman, Manoah's wife, telling her she would be the mother of a son who would take a perpetual Nazarite vow. The messenger of God said, "Now therefore beware, I pray thee, and drink not wine nor strong drink, and eat not any unclean thing: For, lo, thou shalt conceive, and bear a son; and no razor shall come on his head: for the child shall be a Nazarite unto God from the womb: and he shall begin to deliver Israel out of the hand of the Philistines" (Judges 13:4-5).

Samson wasn't the entire answer, yet he was called to "begin to deliver" Israel from bondage.

CONSECRATION AND SEPARATION

The focus on Samson's hair was not to indicate his strength was due to some magical potion. There is nothing superstitious attached to the Word of God.

Instead, the growth of his locks represented his Nazarite vow of consecration. We first read of this in the book of Numbers: "He shall separate himself from wine and strong drink...[and] All the days of the vow of his separation there shall no razor come upon his head: until the days be fulfilled" (Numbers 6:3,5).

Samson was a sign of separation in an apathetic generation.

Dr. Michelle Corral

The usual duration of this vow was 30 days, but in Samson's case it was different. First, his mother took the Nazarite vow during the time the child was in her womb, because from the moment of his conception, Samson was called to be separated unto the Lord--not just for one month, rather for his entire life!

> *MC+*
>
> *Samson was called to be separated unto the Lord — not just for one month, rather for his entire life!*

This fact is important because Samson's consecration was a powerful demonstration against the spirit of apathy prevalent in Israel during those days.

He was the one called to break the yoke of the Philistines over Israel.

THE SECRET OF SEPARATION

I want you to see the connection between Samson and Samuel--who was also a lifelong Nazarite.

Hannah, Samuel's mother, voiced this vow to the Lord: "O Lord of hosts, if thou wilt indeed look on the affliction of thine handmaid, and remember me, and not forget thine handmaid, but wilt give unto thine handmaid a man child, then I will give him unto the Lord all the days of his life, and there shall no razor come upon his head" (1 Samuel 1:11).

The secret of separation is the power property of the anointing. For Samson and Samuel the secret of separation and lifelong consecration released and increased the anointing on their lives.

When you are fighting a spirit which has taken your territory--whether your finances, relationships or even your sanity--it's time for spiritual warfare. This always requires a level of separation and consecration beyond the norm. For example, Daniel went on a 21-day fast (Daniel 10:2-3).

God may tell you, "I want you to make a lifelong vow because I have called you to subdue spirits over your generation. You are My Samuel. You are My Samson."

In Samuel's day, when the Lord moved on his behalf, the Philistines had to relinquish the land they had unlawfully subdued. "And the cities which the Philistines had taken from Israel were restored to Israel, from Ekron even unto Gath; and the coasts thereof did Israel deliver out of the hands of the Philistines. And there was peace between Israel and the Amorites" (1 Samuel 7:14).

There is only one reason for the dramatic turnaround. One person—Samuel---was willing to be consecrated and saturated with the anointing of God.

Dr. Michelle Corral

THE SECOND POWER PRINCIPLE:
YOU HAVE A
PROPHECY AND A PROMISE

As priest and prophet over Israel, the nation looked to Samuel for direction and guidance—not just in spiritual matters but regarding leadership. This was evident when King Saul, who was anointed to serve Israel, made the mistake of listening to the people rather than following the Lord.

Saul pleaded with Samuel for forgiveness, but the priest told the king, "I will not return with thee: for thou hast rejected the word of the Lord, and the Lord hath rejected thee from being king over Israel" (1 Samuel 15:26).

Immediately, the Lord told Samuel: "...fill thine horn with oil, and go, I will send thee to Jesse the Bethlehemite: for I have provided me a king among his sons" (1 Samuel 16:1).

When Samuel arrived in Bethlehem and went to Jesse's home, seven of his sons came before the prophet, however, Samuel rejected them all. Then he inquired, "Are there any more sons?"

Jesse told him about David, his youngest, who was out tending sheep. When he arrived home, God told Samuel, "This is the one!"

The Bible states, "Then Samuel took the horn of oil, and anointed him in the midst of his brethren: and the spirit of the Lord came upon David from that day forward" (v.13).

The anointing is always accompanied by a prophecy and a promise.

MC+

The anointing is always accompanied by a prophecy and a promise.

David was given the promise and prophetic word he would someday be king. From that day forward God began to direct him into destiny. He was appointed and anointed as the oil was poured in power upon him.

PENTECOSTAL POWER

I was in my twenties when the Lord began to use me in ministry. Prior to this, I thought I had the anointing but really knew very little pertaining to the power of the Spirit.

The first time I went to a meeting and saw people falling under the power of God, I made the mistake of giving my mother a positive report about the experience and she thought I had gone completely wakko! But once you have been touched by the Holy Spirit there is no turning back—I continued to seek the deeper things of God. I had received the Pentecostal power of God in my life.

Dr. Michelle Corral

"A FLASH OF LIGHTNING"

One of the greatest moments in my spiritual walk was when I visited a Kathryn Kuhlman meeting at the Shrine Auditorium in Los Angeles back in 1971.

I was seated way up in the third balcony when Miss Kuhlman suddenly pointed her finger toward our area and said, "Someone is being healed of blindness."

MC+

Instantly, with my own eyes, I saw a flash of lightning near me.

Instantly, with my own eyes, I saw a flash of lightning near me. The room turned black and I watched as the bright light moved down the aisle and struck a person who exclaimed, "It has to be me!" And a few seconds later came a joyful shout, "I'm healed!"

I not only felt the anointing wash over my body, the Lord graciously showed me what He had planned for my future. God began to work with such power in our family that my own mother began a ministry to reach the nations of the world.

In God's sight, age is not as important as your willingness to listen, hear and follow His call. David was only a young man, but Samuel anointed him as king. From that day forward, he was a chosen vessel in the Kingdom. God

Dr. Michelle Corral

declared, "I have found David the son of Jesse, a man after mine own heart, which shall fulfill all my will" (Acts 13:22).

The Lord also has a promise and a prophecy for you!

THE THIRD POWER PRINCIPLE:
CONFLICT WILL LEAD TO YOUR CONNECTION

You may have to endure a season of trials and tribulations, yet the Word teaches that your relationship with the Father and your access to the anointing involves conflict.

Saul—who eventually became king—had to pass through a painful place. His conflict led him to his connection.

Scripture tells us about Kish, a Benjamite who "...had a son, whose name was Saul, a choice young man, and a goodly: and there was not among the children of Israel a goodlier person than he: from his shoulders and upward he was higher than any of the people" (1 Samuel 9:2).

However, this young man would soon face a dilemma. Little did he know his predicament would lead him to a place of power.

DILEMMA TURNED TO DESTINY

The first story recorded in the Bible concerning Saul involves the fact his father had lost several donkeys and he told his son, "Take one of the servants and start searching for them."

We read how they "...passed through mount Ephraim, and passed through the land of Shalisha, but they found them not: then they passed through the land of Shalim, and there they were not: and he passed through the land of the Benjamites, but they found them not." (1 Samuel 9:4).

Where in the world were those donkeys? All we know is after searching high and low, "they found them not."

Regardless of how frustrating the journey, Saul had a crucial assignment to fulfill. After all, these animals were part of the family's wealth and his father wanted them returned.

These two men trekked up and down the hills of Ephraim, Shalisha and Shalim and throughout the land of Benjamin, yet the elusive donkeys were no where to be found! Little did he know he was on a destination toward destiny.

Dr. Michelle Corral

Purpose Out of Your Pain!

I'm sure you have faced moments when you've complained, "Lord, I'm just too tired to go on, Why do I have to go through such pain and anguish? Why is everything so difficult?"

Hold on! As you will see in the journey of Saul, the Lord uses our struggles for something supernatural—in this case, they led to the most important connection of his life. At a place called Zuph, Saul finally said to his servant, "We'd better head home or my father will stop thinking about the donkeys and start worrying over us!"

But his servant replied, "Behold now, there is in this city a man of God, and he is an honourable man; all that he saith cometh surely to pass: now let us go thither; peradventure he can show us our way that we should go " (1 Samuel 9:6).

The Power of Providence

The Lord was using this servant to pronounce a prophecy over Saul. Yet, there were still questions. Saul wondered, "If we do meet him, what gift can we offer? We don't even have any more food in our sacks."

The servant replied, "Behold, I have here at hand the fourth part of a Shekel of silver: that will I give to the man of God, to tell us our way. (Beforetime in Israel, when a man went to inquire of God, thus he spake, Come, and let us go to the seer: for he that is now called a Prophet was beforetime called a Seer) "(vv.89).

"Good," said Saul, "Let's go and find this man of God."

As they entered the town, they were noticed by the prophet—none other than Samuel! The power of providence directed him to destiny. God was using conflict to lead him to his connection.

A TURN-AROUND TOMORROW

Even more amazing is the fact that the day before, the Lord revealed to Samuel, "Tomorrow about this time I will send thee a man out of the land of Benjamin, and thou shalt anoint him to be captain over my people Israel, that he may save my people out of the hand of the Philistines: for I have looked upon my people, because their cry is come unto me " (v. 16).

You see, the nation had no leader at this time and Samuel had been commissioned by God to find the right man.

When Samuel caught sight of Saul, the Almighty said to him, "Behold the man whom I spake to thee of! This same shall reign over my people" (v.17).

Saul, still not knowing exactly who he was looking for, stopped the man at the gate of the city and asked, "Tell me, I pray thee, where the seer's house is "(v. 18).

What a surprise when Samuel replied, "I am the seer: go up before me unto the high place; for ye shall eat with me to da y, and tomorrow I will let thee go, and will tell thee all that is in thine heart"(v.l9).

THE "DESTINY DESIGNER"

It was more than mere coincidence! If Saul had not been searching for those lost animals he would have never encountered Samuel. God had everything pre-arranged. He was in the hands of the Destiny Designer!

In Hebrew there is no such word as "had" applied to the children of God. In our language we talk about situations being horrible, even evil. Yet there is never a time when you serve the Lord where things are "rah"—the Hebrew word for evil.

We might be cast down, but not forsaken. We may be persecuted, yet not destroyed. God's presence is always with us.

MC+

We might be cast down, but not forsaken

In the last chapter we spoke of Joseph, however, his being sold into slavery was not "rah." Despite the wickedness of his brothers, the Almighty did not allow evil to affect him. Just the opposite, when Joseph was in the house of Potiphar, the Bible says, "And the Lord was with Joseph, and he was a prosperous man" (Genesis 39:2).

Pressed for the Power of God

Saul was being pressed into a greater level of faith. He was still unaware his difficulty would lead to his anointing and destiny.

After meeting Samuel, Saul, his servant and 30 invited guests had a special meal together. The next morning, as they were about to leave the city, Samuel said to Saul, "Bid the servant pass on before us, (and he passed on,) but stand thou still a While, that I ma y show thee the word of God" (1 Samuel 9:27).

Then Samuel, the prophet of the Most High God, "...took a vial of oil, and poured it upon his head, and kissed him, and said, Is it not because the Lord hath anointed thee to be captain over his inheritance?" (1 Samuel 10:1).

Samuel continued, "And by the way, don't worry about your donkeys. They have been found!" (v.2).

Dr. Michelle Corral

Through the anointing, Saul became King of Israel. Hallelujah! In all those days of searching he was being pressed for the power of God.

YOUR DAY OF DESTINY

You may feel your last hope is ebbing away and you're not sure how much longer you can continue. Perhaps you have been seeking for answers and finding none. You don't realize you are being pressed for the power of God.

Don't be discouraged and give up! God knows precisely where you are and is addressing your problem. He has a plan for your future and one day soon you will feast at His banqueting table. All of your pain is for a purpose.

Beloved, on the authority of God's Word, I want you to know that your painful place will press you into a prosperous future. Your dilemma will be used for destiny.

One day you will look back and rejoice, "Isn't it amazing how the Lord works? He used my dilemma to bring about my deliverance! And it was all for His honor and glory." He is my Destiny Designer.

When you are caught up in the anointing, your problems fade away. He is about to bring you from the brink to a breakthrough. He will use your distress for your success!

The anointing is the spoil for all of your toil. He desires to give you double for your shame (Isaiah 61:7).

The donkeys you were searching for have been found! Conflict will lead you to your connection.

THE FOURTH POWER PRINCIPLE:

THE ANOINTING IS ACCESSED IN THE PLACE OF HIS PRESENCE

Samuel is the most renowned Levite in all of Scripture.

MC+

"If You will grant my prayer, I will give the boy to You."

For years, a barren woman named Hannah fasted, prayed and spent every moment possible at the temple asking God to give her a son. She promised the Lord, "If You will grant my prayer, I will give the boy to You."

By a miracle, Samuel was born and Hannah fulfilled her vow. When the son was weaned, she took him to the temple where he was to live permanently. She said, "Therefore also I have lent him to the Lord; as long as he liveth he shall be lent to the Lord"(1 Samuel 1:28).

From that day forward Samuel lived in the atmosphere of the anointing. As he grew, he became an assistant to the high priest, Eli. He was an attendant to the anointing.

Scripture tells us, "And the child Samuel ministered unto the Lord before Eli. And the word of the Lord was precious in those days; there was no open vision. And it came to pass at that time, when Eli was laid down in his place, and his eyes began to wax dim, that he could not see; And ere the lamp of God went out in the temple of the Lord, where the ark of God was, and Samuel was laid down to sleep " (1 Samuel 3:l-3).

The word "child" is translated as "servant." The temple is where Samuel was first going to hear the Word of the Lord--and in that context he was a child.

ATTENDANTS TO THE ANOINTING

As a servant to Eli, he waited on the man of God and actually "took care" of the anointing and never left his post. Samuel slept in the place of the presence of the Almighty--right next to the Ark of the Covenant! He accessed the anointing through attending the anointing.

Throughout Scripture we read of those who became such attendants. When God spoke to Moses face to face, "...his servant Joshua, the son of Nun, a young man, departed not out of the tabernacle" (Exodus 33:11). Even when Moses was called up into the mountain to receive the commandments of the Lord, Scripture records, "Moses rose up, and his minister Joshua: and Moses went up into the mount of God " (Exodus 24:13).

Because of his lifelong service to Eli, Samuel paid the price for his anointing. The day finally arrived when "...all Israel from Dan even to Beersheha knew that Samuel was established to be a prophet of the Lord" (1 Samuel 3:20).

Before this, he was seen as Eli's attendant, but his loyalty and faithfulness allowed him to receive the promise of God. He was proven to be worthy to represent the Almighty. He accessed the anointing in sacrificial service to Eli.

What a contrast between Eli's spiritual son, Samuel, and his physical sons, Hophni and Phinehas--who rebelled against the Lord and corrupted the priesthood.

It was only Samuel who accessed the anointing.

Dr. Michelle Corral

THE FIFTH POWER PRINCIPLE:
YOUR DESTINY IS DELIVERED THROUGH THE POWER OF PRAYER

The great prophets of God in Scripture were mighty men of prayer. When the enemies of Israel approached, Samuel said, "Gather all Israel...and I will pray for you unto the Lord" (1 Samuel 7:5). The Bible records, "Samuel cried unto the Lord for Israel; and the Lord heard him" (v.9).

Even in the latter years of his life, Samuel declared, "God forbid that I should sin against the Lord in ceasing to pray for you" (1 Samuel 12:23).

David wrote, "Moses and Aaron [were] among his priests, and Samuel [was] among them that call upon his name; they called upon the Lord, and he answered them" (Psalm 99:6).

Jeremiah states that the true test of a prophet is his prayer life: "But if they be prophets, and if the word of the Lord be with them, let them now make intercession to the Lord of hosts" (Jeremiah 27:18).

When you discover the Samuel Secret:

Dr. Michelle Corral

- ❖ You will reclaim lost territory.
- ❖ You will have a prophecy and a promise.
- ❖ Your conflict will lead to your connection.
- ❖ Your anointing will be found in the place of His presence.
- ❖ Your destiny will be delivered through prayer.

The power principles of God's Word will be yours!

Chapter Six

The Elijah Element

When a prophet is introduced in Scripture it is usually accompanied by his pedigree from which we learn facts about his past. For example:

- ❖ Jeremiah was "...the son of Hilkiah, of the priests that were in Anathoth in the land of Benjamin" (Jeremiah 1:1).
- ❖ Zephaniah was "...the son of Cushi; the son of Gedaliah, the son of Amariah, the son of Hizkiah" (Zephanaih 1:1).
- ❖ Zechariah was "...the son of Berechiah, the son of Iddo the prophet"(Zechariah 1:1).

It was a pattern in Hebrew Scripture that if your father was a prophet you would likely follow in his footsteps--thus the term "sons of the prophets."

But when it comes to the man who has been designated as one of the greatest prophets of Bible times--Elijah--we find his credentials are derived from an entirely different source. This revered man of God was who he was because of his close relationship with the Almighty, although Scripture does not pronounce his pedigree.

HIDING AND ABIDING PRAYER

Elijah gained his position by hiding and abiding in prayer-- what I call "The Elijah Element."

Here's how Scripture introduces him: "And Elijah the Tish bite, who was of the inhabitants of Gilead, said unto Ahab, As the Lord God of Israel liveth, before whom I stand, there shall not be dew nor rain these years, but according to my word. And the word of the Lord came unto him, saying, Get thee hence, and turn thee eastward, and hide thyself by the brook Cherith, that is before Jordan" (1 Kings 17:1-3).

We know where he came from, but nothing about his family. Instead, Elijah's ministry was birthed when God told him to "hide" at a brook near the river Jordan. Elijah began to hide and abide in God.

BEYOND THE PRAYER OF PETITION

There are many forms of prayer, and each has a valid purpose. They include:

- ❖ Thanksgiving declaring our gratitude for God's blessings.
- ❖ Petition--asking the Lord for what we need.
- ❖ Adoration--expressing our love to the Father.
- ❖ Forgiveness--requesting the Lord's mercy.
- ❖ Agreement--believing together for a mountain to be moved.
- ❖ Intercession--a prayer to the Lord on behalf of a person or situation.

In this chapter, however, I want you to see another dimension of prayer. It involves dwelling in the presence of the Living God and becoming the habitation of heaven.

THE MIRACLES MULTIPLIED

The "hiding and abiding" prayer experienced by Moses, Elijah and the Son of God can be yours. It is where the power of the Almighty is released and increased into your life.

One of the secrets of the powerful ministry of Jesus on earth was the fact He continually pulled Himself away from the throngs and found a place of seclusion, a place alone to talk with His Father. For example, "And it came to pass about an eight days after these sayings, he took Peter and John and James, and went up into a mountain to pray. And as he prayed, the fashion of his countenance was altered, and his raiment was white and glistering. And, behold, there talked with him two men, which were Moses and Elias [Elijah]" (Luke 9:28-30).

> *MC+*
> *When Jesus and the disciples came down from the mountain, the miracles multiplied!*

When Jesus and the disciples came down from the mountain, the miracles multiplied! The context conveys it was because Jesus sought the solitude of hiding and abiding prayer.

THE PREFACE TO POWER

God's first directive to Elijah was to "...turn thee eastward, and hide thyself by the brook" (1 Kings 17:1-3).

There is always an order of events in God's Word chronological sense of Scripture. What precedes and follows is essential---and what happens first is the reason for the eventual outcome.

Elijah didn't begin his ministry by raising the widow's son from the dead or calling fire down from heaven. The signs and wonders came later. He started by getting alone with God.

The word "hide" is like a punctuation point the Lord is emphasizing. In that quiet place near the brook Cherith, the Almighty directed and perfected Elijah's call. It was the preface to the power of a prophetic life.

REKINDLED AND RESTORED

Perhaps you are at a crossroads where you need to see a "dead" dream rekindled or a relationship restored. It may be that the prophecy you have been living off of for the last twenty years needs to be reconfirmed.

Beloved, if you are longing to see an open heaven instead of a closed door, start this minute to activate the Elijah Element. Begin hiding and abiding in the presence of the Almighty.

As the apostle Paul writes: "For ye are dead, and your life is hid with Christ in God" (Colossians 3:3).

Prayer must be a priority--not something you try to cram into your hectic schedule. Your calendar must be dominated and consecrated by your relationship with the Father. The cry of your heart should be, "I hunger and thirst for You, Lord. And I cannot exist one day without You."

This advanced form of prayer is only possible when love calls you into communion with Him. You tell the Lord, "You are my other self--and I love you with all my mind, soul and strength. I give myself completely to You."

Dr. Michelle Corral

YOUR LEVEL OF LOVE

Some people only approach the Lord when they have a particular need. Then, when God answers, the communication ceases.

If human wants and desires are the only motivation, the level of your prayer is elementary. That's why I am asking you to spend as long is it takes with Jesus until you fall in love with Him.

Certainly you will endure "dry "periods when your mind wanders or you can't seem to break through the clouds of heaven. But in those times your faith must rise until you "pray through" and touch the Lord once more. He is waiting for your worship, adoration and undivided attention.

FILLING UP WITH FIRE

Without a prayer life your ministry cannot become prophetic. Programs are wonderful, but your future will only be transformed when you learn how to hide and abide in God.

The Lord didn't tell Elijah, "Let me show you how to build a program so you can do away with the spirit of Jezebel." Instead, He told the prophet, "I want to take you to a quiet place--where My anointing will rest upon you to such an extent that when you begin to represent Me on earth, the world will tremble and know I am God."

POSSESSING THE PROMISES

Many don't have a clear understanding of what it means to live the "prophetic life." It involves:

- ❖ Being sensitive and in touch with what is taking place in heaven as it pertains to earth.
- ❖ Possessing the promises of God.
- ❖ Living in the realm of what has been spoken over your life.
- ❖ Fighting principalities and powers.

Prophecy itself is only one small element of the life we are discussing--and it not the result of reading a book on the topic or even meeting an individual who has this particular gift of the Spirit.

The prophetic life comes to those who cannot exist outside the habitation of heaven. It is your home, and where you reside.

THE CALL TO BE CRUCIFIED

In my personal communion with the Father, I spend at least the first two hours of my prayer time each week making sure my human will is absolutely put to death. I pray, "God, I want you to destroy anything that is of me."

My objective is to be filled with God, not with Michelle Corral. That's why I must be crucified in the prayer closet so I will hear what the Lord has to say. I must be directed and perfected by Him.

MC+
Prayer advances your soul closer to the God who gave you breath and life.

Prayer advances your soul closer to the God who gave you breath and life. It's not just shouts of praise and saying "Hallelujah." Rather, it involves your very being coming into union with the Father and becoming one with Him.

This union can only take place when God consumes the vessel--and this is impossible if the vessel is filled with self.

The only way the Lord can bring you into a place of great power and authority is if your will is totally removed and His will is preeminent.

THE SHELTER OF THE SECRET PLACE

If you were to personally ask Jesus where to pray, here is what He would tell you: "But thou, when thou prayest, enter into thy closet, and when thou hast shut thy door, pray to thy Father which is in secret; and thy Father which seeth in secret shall reward thee openly" (Matthew 6:6).

Don't just go into your closet, "shut the door." In other words, find a place alone where there are no distractions or interruptions.

The psalmist knew the importance of finding that "secret place" with the Lord:

- ❖ "He that dwelleth in the secret place of the most High shall abide under the shadow of the Almighty" (Psalm 91:1).
- ❖ "...hide me under the shadow of thy wings" (Psalm 17:8).
- ❖ "Thou art my hiding place and my shield" (Psalm 119:114).
- ❖ "Thou shalt hide them in the secret of thy presence" (Psalm 31:20)

When we are hidden in prayer, there is safety and protection. The Lord becomes your shield.

It is also the key to answered prayer. Jesus says, "If ye abide in me, and my words abide in you, ye shall ask what ye will, and it shall be done unto you" (John 15:7). It is the hiding and abiding Elijah Element.

Dr. Michelle Corral

THE BURNING BUSH

Elijah was not the only prophet to employ the element of hiding and abiding with God. Moses also understood what it meant to be in the secret place of the Most High God.

The Almighty's first conversation with Moses was not in the hustle and bustle of Egypt, but out in the middle of nowhere near the mount of Horeb on "the backside of the desert" (Exodus 3:1).

There was a reason he was able to challenge Pharaoh and bring down witchcraft in the land of Egypt. It was a nation controlled and dominated by the occult--a place of pyramids and symbol worship.

How could one man have the power to release the children of Israel after 400 years of generational bondage? It was because he learned to dwell in the habitation of heaven- and how to hide himself in God.

GLIMPSING THE GLORY

Even during the years of wanderings in the wilderness, the Almighty continued to call Moses away from the children of Israel and speak with him personally. On one occasion, the Lord said, "Behold, there is a place by me, and thou shalt stand upon a rock: And it shall come to pass, While my glory passeth by, that I Will put thee in clift of the rock, and will cover thee with my hand while I pass by" (Exodus 33:21-22).

If God had not prepared such a hiding place for Moses, the presence of the Lord would have been far too powerful. God told him, "Thou canst not see my face: for there shall no man see me, and live" (v.20).

M&+

Moses met the Father-and was covered with His hand.

Moses met the Father-and was covered with His hand.

FALLING AT HIS FEET

Are you ready for a personal encounter with God? If so, be prepared for the unexpected!

One day, the Lord spoke to the prophet Ezekiel, asking him to go to a certain place where they could talk. As he describes the experience, "Then I arose, and went forth into the plain: and, behold, the glory of the Lord stood there, as the glory which I saw by the river of Chebar: and I fell on my face. Then the spirit entered into me, and set me upon my feet, and spake with me, and said unto me, Go, shut thyself Within thine house" (Ezekiel 3:23-24).

The glory of God was so awesome that the prophet literally fell to the ground.

When we praise the Lord we raise our hands, and in worship we are in reverence, but when the glory falls we are speechless, all we can do is behold Him and fall before Him.

John was in the Spirit when he had a revelation of Jesus. He writes: "And when I saw him, I fell at his feet as dead" (Revelation 1:17). The reason John could make such a statement is because glory always kills the flesh.

THE SILENCE OF THE SPIRIT

In Kathryn Kuhlman's meetings, when the glory of the Lord would descend, you could hear a pin drop. In that sacred atmosphere people were being delivered and sick bodies healed.

You see, there is a difference between quietness and silence. Quietness has to do with the flesh--a deliberate act of our will. But silence is of the Spirit--when man is immobilized in the presence of the Living God. At that moment we are under the subjection and submission of the Holy Spirit and the glory has taken control.

After Ezekiel fell on his face before the Lord, the Spirit entered into him and raised him to his feet. Then God gave the prophet the most important direction of all: "Go, shut thyself within thine house" (Ezekiel 3:24).

The Lord was saying, "I plan to use you in a mighty way, but before I do, you need to get alone with Me."

It was a call to hide and abide in God.

ALONE NEAR THE THRONE

Shut the door! Enter into your closet! Find a place of solitude with God and let Him feed you and reveal His next assignment. He will answer all those questions

MC+

Shut the door! Enter into your closet!

you've been worrying over and pull back the curtain so you can see His marvelous vision for your future.

At such a time, your petition becomes secondary, but if you remember and say, "Lord, I forgot to ask You"--He will reply:

- ❖ "Don't worry My child, I've already taken care of it."
- ❖ "The moment you came into this secret place, I healed your son."
- ❖ "I solved that financial problem."
- ❖ "I restored your broken relationship."

Dr. Michelle Corral

"Turn Thee Eastward"

At the start of this chapter, in the passage, which includes the Elijah Element of hiding and abiding, there are three significant words which should not be overlooked. God told the prophet: "turn thee eastward" (1 Kings 17:3).

One of the ways we interpret Scripture is called "marking the match"--or using a comparative connection from another word or passage. This methodology is referred to in Hebrew as "remez," meaning, "to allude to."

Jeremiah is the author of first and second Kings, which detail the events that took place in the life of Elijah. The phrase "turn thee eastward" matches language used in other parts of Hebrew Scripture so those making an exegetical study will know that God is not just referring to a particular direction. There is something more to the meaning.

MC+

"Eastward" represents the habitation of heaven on earth.

Turn to the first book of the Bible and you will see that "eastward" represents the habitation of heaven on earth. Scripture records, "And the Lord God planted a garden eastward in Eden; and there he put the man whom he had formed" (Genesis 2:8).

We also read: "So he drove out the man; and he placed at the east of the garden of Eden Cherubims, and a flaming sword which tuned every way, to keep the way of the tree of life" (Genesis 3:24).

Eastward represents the Holy of Holies.

THE GATES OF GLORY

When God tells us where to hide and abide, He is giving us directions to the entrance of God's glory to earth. This is exactly what Eden was--the place where the Creator descended from heaven to deal with man. It was there Adam and Eve "...heard the voice of the Lord God walking in the garden in the cool of the day" (Genesis 3:8).

Eden was the tabernacle of God on earth. And when you come into that secret place you are dwelling at the gates of glory. So when the Lord tells you to turn eastward, it's not according to the compass, but toward the direction of the entrance to the habitation of heaven on earth.

By saying "Turn eastward," God is literally giving you the blessing in advance. And if you do what the Lord commands, you will experience the gates of glory in your prayer closet.

Here is the testimony of Ezekiel: "Afterward he brought me to the gate, even the gate that looketh to ward the east:

Dr. Michelle Corral

And, behold, the glory of the God of Israel came from the way of the east: and his voice was like a noise of man y waters: and the earth shined with his glory" (Ezekiel 43:1-2).

Once more "east" represents an entry into glory--the place where God meets with man.

TIME TO TURN

Just as Jeremiah used "eastward" in Kings to allude to the Garden of Eden, there is a comparative connection in the use of the word "turn." It not only means moving in a new direction or "coming close," it also refers to the seeking and speaking principle of prayer.

During Moses' call to ministry, an angel of the Lord appeared to him in flames of fire from within a bush. But even though the bush was on fire, it didn't burn.

Moses said, "I will now turn aside, and see this great sight, Why the bush is not burnt. And when the Lord saw that he turned aside to see, God called unto him out of the midst of the bush, and said, Moses, Moses. And he said, Here am I" (Exodus 3:1-4).

Please realize that Moses is the author of his own text regarding how these events happened. It is evident that he would have missed his moment had he not turned aside to see what was taking place.

QUESTIONS FOR MOSES

If you were to interview Moses, perhaps you would ask:

- ❖ What was it like when God called you? How did it feel?
- ❖ How did you come into such phenomenal power?
- ❖ How did you reach the place where you could challenge the darkness of Egypt and call down the power of heaven?

If Moses were here, he would tell you, "When I saw the fire leaping out of that bush I had to stop taking care of my sheep and find out what was taking place." But it wasn't the bush nor the fire that called him to lead God's people out of bondage.

Here is the most important part of the story. Scripture says, "And when the Lord saw that he turned aside to see..." (v.4).

The test was in Moses' willingness to turn. It was only then "God called unto him." He turned aside to seek God.

SEEKING AND SPEAKING

How about you? Are you willing to make that life changing turn?

Your "burning bush" may be the quickening of the Spirit or a word spoken in a church service you attended. Perhaps it appeared in a vision or a dream--or what the Lord has placed in your heart.

MC+

God is waiting to see if you are willing to turn toward Him.

God is waiting to see if you are willing to turn toward Him. It may be three o'clock in the morning when the Lord whispers, "Will you spend an hour with Me in prayer?"

The Lord is saying to you even now, "It is when you seek that I will speak."

If you are obedient to turn, He will tell you everything you need to know and show you a revelation of Himself. Then, when you see who He is, you will know who you truly are!

Claim the heritage, which is rightfully yours. What the Lord has done in times past He will do for you today.

Listen for God's instructions and add the Elijah Element. Start hiding and abiding in Him.

Chapter Seven

Sensitivity To The Spirit

Rees Howells, a coal miner from Wales, became known as The Apostle of Intercessory Prayer.

He was a product of the great Welsh Revival at the turn of the Twentieth Century, which spread throughout England and to many nations of the world. It sparked the 1906 Azusa Street Revival in Los Angeles, which birthed a tremendous spiritual awakening in America.

Howells taught there is a huge difference between a prayer warrior and an intercessor.

A prayer warrior is a faithful person who will call on God for as long as it takes to see the answer come to pass. The intercessor, however, is involved in abiding prayer, asking, "How do I constrain the presence of God over this prayer request?"

Howells writings teach that if there is a prayer request, the person bringing the need before the Lord must gain the right, the authority and position to become an intercessor in the matter.

He emphasized the point that there are two intercessors. The first is Jesus, who at this very moment is in heaven, seated at the right hand of the Father, and He "...ever liveth to make intercession" for you (Hebrews 7:25).

The other is the Holy Spirit, who is on earth, seeking a vessel He might be an intercessor through. Scripture tells us, "Likewise the Spirit also helpeth our infirmities: for we know not what we should pray for as we ought: but the Spirit itself maketh intercession for us with groanings which cannot be uttered" (Romans 8:26).

The person the Holy Spirit is seeking is one who will go beyond being a prayer warrior and become a true intercessor.

A man or woman does not gain spiritual authority and position by just saying, "I am a believer and now I am going to take my place in God." It requires much more.

FROM BURDEN TO BLESSING

When Rees Howells began his ministry of intercession he learned of a woman who died of tuberculosis. The father was a drunkard and the children left behind were virtually homeless.

In prayer, Howells told God, "I have a great burden for these children."

The Lord responded, "If you have such a concern and are willing to pray for them, what are you willing to do for them?"

He said, "I am prepared to give them some of my money."

During the next several weeks, every time Howells prayed, it seemed there was a battle waging between himself and the Holy Spirit and he could feel an actual "pulling" of the Spirit regarding the matter. Finally, he said to himself, "All right, if I am really going to take my authority and my prayer position, I must be willing to raise these children myself."

At that moment he was no longer just a prayer warrior on behalf of the need; he became an intercessor, saying, "Regardless of the price, I even offer my body to You if that is what it takes to answer this request."

He was tested. At the beginning he was giving money every week from his meager paycheck to feed these children, but now he made the decision to adopt them. Later, after the test, the aunt of the children stepped in and adopted them.

THE POWER OF POSITION

As an intercessor you know the prayer need is accomplished either by the physical evidence or by the presence of God breaking out in such as way that every time you pray or even think about the need, you feel the anointing of the Holy Spirit.

By deciding to provide for and raise these children, Rees Howells gained his authority and position with God.

From that point forward, every time he prayed for an orphan or a child in need, he had the right to go before God.

MC+

Abiding prayer means to stay in the presence of the Lord until the anointing brings the assurance of the answer.

Abiding prayer means to stay in the presence of the Lord until the anointing brings the assurance of the answer. At times it may require weeks of fasting as the Spirit tells you, "This is how we are going to constrain the anointing over your prayer request." In other instances, He may instruct you, "Pray at least three hours every night on behalf of the need."

INTERCESSION FOR INDIA

One day Rees Howells was interceding for the newly emancipated women in India who had virtually no food and their children were starving to death. So he asked the Lord, "How am I going to constrain your anointing over this prayer?"

God clearly told him, "For the next 40 days I want you to live exactly how the poor exist in India and eat only one bowl of rice each day."

He obeyed the Lord, even though his family and those in the village where he lived thought he had lost his mind. But miraculously, after 40 days, a law was passed in the parliament of India to protect the women who had been liberated in that nation.

"REMOVE YOUR HAT"

In the social culture of the times of Rees Howells, a Welsh gentleman wouldn't even think of leaving his home without wearing a hat-even if you worked in a coal mine making just a few pence each day.

One evening, while interceding before the Lord on behalf of a particular need, God said to Howells, "You know, when you come into the sanctuary or bow your head to pray, you

Dr. Michelle Corral

remove your hat." Then He added, "If you are going to be abiding, I want you to be hatless for a few weeks."

So the next morning he told his mother, "Don't prepare my hat today." She would always make sure it was brushed and perfect before he left the house. When he told her why, she was even more puzzled. And on the streets, people thought he was crazy.

During this period, he received an invitation to go to London, where it was unthinkable to be without a hat. But the Holy Spirit questioned, "Are you willing to obey me regarding this matter?"

The answer was "Yes."

If the Lord told him to take off his shoes for a week, he was ready to obey if that's what it took to maintain the presence of God over a prayer request.

FROM ABILITY TO AUTHORITY

We need to thank God for mighty prayer warriors who spend countless hours before the throne on behalf of an urgent need. But the church requires more intercessors-- those who have earned their authority and position and have a deep relationship with the Holy Spirit.

Only when you have given yourself completely to Him as a vessel can you ask, "What kind of groanings do you want to come forth from me? What kind of birth and travail does it take in my life for this miracle to happen?"

RELEASING AND INCREASING SENSITIVITY TO GOD IN OUR PRAYER

On Mount Carmel there was a great demonstration of the power of God. On one side 450 prophets of Baal had prayed to their gods in an attempt to call fire down from heaven and consume a sacrifice. Yet nothing happened.

On the other side was just one man--the prophet Elijah--who prayed, "Lord God of Abraham, Isaac, and of Israel, let it be known this day that thou art God in Israel, and that I am thy servant, and that I have done all these things at thy word" (1 Kings 18:36).

Suddenly the fire fell and the amazed onlookers knew who was the true and Living God.

MC+
Suddenly the fire fell and the amazed onlookers knew who was the true and Living God.

Immediately following this victory, another miracle occurred in the life of Elijah. It contains a powerful lesson for us today-four vital steps to releasing and increasing your sensitivity to God in prayer:

STEP NUMBER ONE:
BE SENSITIVE TO THE
SOUND OF THE SPIRIT

After the triumph at Mount Carmel, Elijah said to Ahab, "Get thee up, eat and drink; for there is a sound of abundance rain" (1 Kings 18:41).

This was an incredible statement, especially since Israel had been suffering from a drought for three years. The land was parched and so dry that animals were dying and people were famished.

In the natural there was no sight or sound of rain--not a cloud in the sky or the hint of thunder in the distance.

MC+
Have you ever heard something in your spirit, which was completely contrary to your current situation?

Have you ever heard something in your spirit, which was completely contrary to your current situation?

Perhaps you were in prayer and the Lord said, "I am going to heal you"--but the miracle didn't happen. Or the Lord declared, "I will open this door," yet it remained closed. You were confident you heard from God in your spirit.

In an earth that was silent, Elijah heard the refreshing sound of the abundance of rain. The Lord was fine-tuning a spiritual sensitivity he would use more than once. Later, when the prophet was standing on the side of a mountain, the Lord passed by and there was a great wind, an earthquake and a fire, but the Bible says the Lord was not in any of those things. How did God speak to Elijah? Through "a still small voice" (1 Kings 19:12).

The reason the prophet was able to hear the Lord was because he had a special sensitivity to the sound of the Spirit. At that moment, God gave Elijah specific directions for his future ministry. This sensitivity was fruit of the hiding and abiding Elijah Element of prayer.

SUDDENLY--A SOUND!

Are your ears attuned to hear from above? Just before Jesus returned to heaven, He told the believers to gather in Jerusalem and wait for the promised Holy Spirit. On the Day of Pentecost, 120 were quietly praying in the Upper Room, when "...suddenly there came a sound from heaven as of a rushing mighty wind" (Acts 2:2). The Spirit descended with power!

Much earlier, in the desert, Elijah was able to hear the sound of rain in a dry, parched land. The anointing was released and increased on his spiritual ears.

Dr. Michelle Corral

STEP NUMBER TWO:
MOVE WHAT YOU HEAR INTO MOTION

Elijah didn't just hear the sound of rain and keep the matter secretly to himself, he told someone about it! Immediately, he called out to Ahab, "Get thee up, eat and drink; for there is a sound of abundance of rain" (1 Kings 18:41). He said this by faith according to the sound he heard by the Spirit.

By this statement the prophet placed what the Spirit said and moved it into motion.

When was the last time you spoke what you heard in your inner man? The Lord may have told you details concerning your job, but others laughed you to scorn. However, there is a reason God asked you to speak out. He knows you will need a witness when victory finally arrives. As you hear the sounds by the Spirit, you must move it into motion.

Far too many Christians keep their spiritual life completely to themselves. When God gives them a clear directive of what they are to be doing in the Kingdom, they say, "I'm just going to wait on the Lord to see if this really happens." And they don't share it with one soul.

That's not God's pattern for triumph. He expects you to declare the dream, even to "Write the Vision, and make it plain upon tables, that he that readeth it" (Habahkuk 2:2)"

This does not mean you get ahead of God. However, when He places something in your soul, move it into motion. This is how you propel what is prophetic into position.

ME+
When He places something in your soul, move it into motion. This is how you propel what is prophetic into position.

A DIRECTIVE TO "DO!"

It is easy to say, "God gave me a revelation of what is going to take place," yet what did you do about it. Have you obeyed the Spirit of God when He says "Start working until the vision is accomplished"?

We have a responsibility to go beyond thoughts or intentions. After Paul tells us to think on what is true, honest, just, pure, lovely and of good report, he says, "Those things, which ye have both learned, and received, and heard, and seen in me, do: and the God of peace shall be with you" (Philippians 4:9).

Dr. Michelle Corral

In other words, put it into action! Remember, to whom much is given, much is required (Luke 12:48).

STEP NUMBER THREE:
PRESS YOUR PRAYER
TO A PROPHETIC LEVEL

Elijah didn't just hear the sound of rain in his spirit and move it into motion by speaking it in faith, he took the next step of pressuring it in prayer. This is what elevated him into the prophetic--the level where miracles occur. It is the level where the Spirit saturates prayer.

According to Scripture, the prophet, "...went up to the top of Carmel; and he cast himself down upon the earth, and put his face between his knees" (1 Kings 17:42). By faith, he pressed what he heard into a prophetic level of prayer.

MC+
Since God gave Elijah the sound of rain by the Spirit, it was time to pray for a downpour!

So what if it's 95 degrees and the earth is cracked and parched? Since God gave Elijah the sound of rain by the Spirit, it was time to pray for a downpour!

He acted while the revelation was fresh, saying, "If I wait until tomorrow, the anointing on the sound I heard may be gone. I've got to pray now!"

Inaction will cause the intensity and propensity for the miracle to dissipate.

Elijah's prayer for rain became completely coerced and immersed by the Spirit of God, and "...as many as are led by the Spirit of God, they are the sons of God" (Romans 8:14).

Instead of praying your own prayer, wait for the Spirit to show you how to pray (Romans 8:26). "And he that searcheth the hearts knoweth what is the mind of the Spirit, because he maketh intercession for the saints according to the will of God " (v.27).

When you pray in the Holy Ghost, you are dangerous to the devil. He would rather have you spend hours rebuking him than to have one word come out of your mouth, which is Spirit--anointed.

This is what is meant by pressing prayer into a prophetic level.

THE GIVER OF GIFTS

We are counseled to be "...building up yourselves on your most holy faith, praying in the Holy Ghost" (Jude 1:20).

One of the scriptural gifts of the Spirit is tongues, but Paul says, "I will pray with the spirit, and I will pray with the understanding also" (1 Corinthians 14:15). This is possible by interpreting our own tongues--and if you do not have this gift, ask the Spirit. Remember, "...ye have not, because ye ask not" (James 4:2).

If the interpretation of tongues was not necessary for your spiritual life, God would not have included it in the array of the gifts of the Holy Spirit (1 Corinthians 12 :10).

The Father desires that you understand the deep things of God. In these days we need to depend on the supernatural and have all the gifts working in our lives--not only tongues and their interpretation, but, the word of wisdom, the word of knowledge, faith, healing, the working of miracles, prophecy and the discerning of spirits.

Elijah became an *intercessor* as the Spirit moved his prayer to a prophetic level.

STEP NUMBER FOUR:
DEFINE AND ALIGN WHAT YOU HEARD FROM HEAVEN

The prophet heard the sound, spoke through faith and pressed the matter before God in prayer. But there was one last step which was necessary--he needed someone to stand with him in agreement.

With sky-high expectation, Elijah said to his servant, *"Go up now, look toward the sea. And he went up, and looked, and said, There is nothing"* (1 Kings 17:43).

What a crushing blow that must have been to the prophet. After God had given him the "sound" of rain, the servant returned with a negative report. This was spiritual warfare!

Elijah was persistent. Seven more times, he asked his assistant to go and look again (v.43).

Surely the Lord had spoken, and now all he needed was for one servant to come into agreement with the word from heaven. As far as the prophet was concerned, he would have sent this young man out 100 times until they were aligned together in agreement.

Delight in a Downpour

Finally, on the seventh try, the servant returned with just a "tiny" praise report: As Scripture describes the scene, *"And it came to pass at the seventh time, that he said, Behold, there ariseth a little cloud out of the sea, like a man's hand"* (v.44).

That's all Elijah needed to hear. Even before there was one drop of rain, he told his servant to run to Ahab with this message: "Hitch up your chariot and head for Jezreel before the rain stops you!" Now that's faith!

Immediately, the miracle happened. *"And came to pass in the mean while, that the heaven was black with clouds and wind, and there was a great rain"* (v.45)

MC+

With agreement came the miracle.

With agreement came the miracle-- not just a fleeting shower, but the heavens opened and a "great" rain flooded the land. They were getting drenched!

If the Lord places a message in your spirit, do not treat it lightly. Be sensitive to the sound of the Spirit, move it into motion, press it to a level that is prophetic and define and align what you heard from heaven.

A FINAL WORD

God opens many wonderful avenues to give you access to the anointing, but there is one you need to continually be sensitive to.

The anointing is released and increased through the means of a mentor. To express it another way: Without a mentor there is no mantle. The mantle prophetically prefigures how the anointing is both contagious and captured.

Almost immediately after Elijah heard the "still small voice" of God on Mount Horeb, he found a young man by the name of Elisha plowing in the fields. Led by the Spirit,

"*Elijah passed by him, and cast his mantle upon him*" (1 Kings 19:19).

What occurred next was just as amazing. The Bible records that Elisha "*...left the oxen, and ran after Elijah, and said, 'Let me, I pray thee, kiss my father and my mother, and then I will follow thee*" (v.20). Then, as a sign of total commitment, Elisha, slaughtered his oxen, set fire to his plowing equipment, fed the people a final barbecue and "*... went after Elijah, and ministered unto him*" (v.21).

Your mantle must be both merited and inherited.

Just before Elijah was taken up to heaven in a whirlwind he asked Elisha three different times to wait behind. But the dedicated assistant to the prophet declared, "*As the Lord liveth, and as thy soul liveth, I will not leave thee*" (2 Kings 2:6).

Then, when the prophet was lifted to heaven, Elisha "*...took the mantle of Elijah that fell from him*" (2 Kings 2:14). The fact Elijah left the mantle behind shows this was bequeathed--an inheritance for Elisha.

After smiting the waters of the Jordan with the mantle and walking across on dry ground, the people exclaimed, "*The spirit of Elijah doth rest on Elisha*" (v.15).

If you are lacking a spiritual mentor in your life from whom you can learn and be accountable, ask the Lord to lead you to such a person. And should you be a mature Christian to whom much has been entrusted, it is your obligation to share the wisdom, knowledge and anointing you have received.

A DIVINE DIMENSION

The Lord has inspired me to share my heart with you so you will personally know what it means to be saturated by the Spirit. My prayer is that you will have continually access to the anointing.

- ❖ Have you walked the avenues of access to the anointing?
- ❖ Are you separated and submitted to the Lord?
- ❖ Are you a servant of the service of God?
- ❖ Have you experienced the empowering effects of the anointing?
- ❖ Have you discovered Samuel's secret to apostolic authority?
- ❖ Will you practice the "Elijah Element" of hiding and abiding in God?
- ❖ Are you sensitive to the Spirit?

Dr. Michelle Corral

Today, I am praying you will become saturated, consecrated and elevated into the very presence of God. May your life be completely surrendered to the Spirit as you access the anointing.

Chapter Eight

Protocols of Power

~A DIFFERENT UNCTION WITH A DIFFERENT FUNCTION ~

In this chapter we will be taking an *in depth* look at the anointing. The first time we see the anointing introduced to us in Scripture, we will not only begin to understand the effects of the anointing but we will also begin to comprehend the differences in the types of anointing that can exist in our lives. During our investigation, we will also analyze the different components that are used to compose each anointing *(oil)* and how these components contribute specifically to their purpose and power.

Beloved, did you know that the anointing has the power to change the substance of a thing? It has the power to bring the manifestation for transformation no matter what it touches. For example, the Bible teaches us

MC+
Did you know that the anointing has the power to change the substance of a thing?

that after the prophet Samuel took the vial of oil and anointed King Saul he was changed into another man.

1 Samuel 10:6,9 KJV
[6] And the Spirit of the Lord will come upon thee, and thou shalt prophesy with them, and shalt be turned into another man. [9] And it was so, that when he had turned his back to go from Samuel, God gave him another heart: and all those signs came to pass that day.

One of the first places the anointing appears in Scripture in the form of oil is when Jacob poured oil over the place where he dreamed the God-given dream for his destiny in Genesis 28:18. The dream that Jacob had was a *nevuah* (prophesy) that came in the form of a vision in the night. The text teaches how he woke out of his sleep and poured oil over the stones he had used for pillows in that place. By pouring oil on the place where he dreamed, he consecrated and separated that place and called it Bethel – The House of God and the gate of heaven.

Genesis 28:17b KJV
This is none other but the house of God, and this is the gate of heaven.

Beforetime, that place was called Luz, which in Hebrew means violence, darkness, and sin. The oil Jacob poured on those stones not only brought about consecration but it also brought about *transformation* to the atmosphere.

Genesis 28:19 KJV
And he called the name of that place Bethel: but the name of that city was called Luz at the first.

Luz during that time was known for being a place of violence and robbery. But when Jacob poured the oil over the ground he consecrated that spot unto the Lord and brought about a divine transformation over the entire territory. Thus, the oil (the anointing) had the power to change the atmosphere of that place from being a place of darkness to a place of destiny.

Another very important place the anointing appears in the form of oil is in the book of Exodus. In a hermeneutical sense of Scripture, the texts we are about to analyze in the book of Exodus from chapters 27-30 could be divided into a prophetic unit, which deals specifically with the anointing. We can name this unit "The Unit on the Anointing" or in a Hebraic sense "Parshah Anointing." The

Dr. Michelle Corral

Book of Exodus in chapters 27-30 prophetically prefigures two types of oil. This unit begins with the *Shemen ha Zayit* (pure olive oil) and ends with *Shemen ha Kadosh* (the holy anointing oil). I call these two types of oil *two types of anointing*. Each category contains a different *unction* for a different *function*. Let's take a look at what the scripture says about these two oils.

Exodus 27:20 KJV
And thou shalt command the children of Israel, that they bring thee pure oil olive beaten for the light, to cause the lamp to burn always.

Exodus 30:22-25, 31 KJV
[22] Moreover the Lord spake unto Moses, saying, [23] Take thou also unto thee principal spices, of pure myrrh five hundred shekels, and of sweet cinnamon half so much, even two hundred and fifty shekels, and of sweet calamus two hundred and fifty shekels, [24] And of cassia five hundred shekels, after the shekel of the sanctuary, and of oil olive an hin: [25] And thou shalt make it an oil of holy ointment, an ointment compound after the art of the apothecary: it shall be an holy anointing oil. [31] And thou shalt speak unto the children of Israel, saying, This shall be an holy anointing oil unto me throughout your generations.
The first oil mentioned is the pure olive oil. The children of Israel were to bring a certain measurement of pure olive oil every day to Moses in the tabernacle, which was "beaten

for the light." Then at the conclusion of this unit of Scripture we see that there is another type of oil mentioned. This *superior substance* of oil, which is spoken of in Exodus 30, contains certain highly valuable spices. It is not just the spices that make this particular oil so important; it is the measurements and contents of each component. The purpose of Scripture here is to separate and consecrate the differences defined between the two types of oil; each oil with a different *unction*, each oil with a different *function*.

Before we begin to discuss these two oils further, we must first understand that these two types of oil are not the same. When we are moving in the Spirit and when we are moving in the realm of the Spirit not everything is the same. We have a tendency to make everything generic. For instance, when we see the word "oil," we tend to only think of one type of oil – the pure olive oil. But when we are dealing with biblical languages, such as Hebrew and Greek, we cannot think that every word has a generic meaning nor can we assume that every word has the same meaning or same purpose. This is a prophetic unit that Scripture has been systematically fixed together, because it has within it a theology of the anointing and it is showing

> *MC+*
>
> *When we are moving in the Spirit and when we are moving in the realm of the Spirit not everything is the same.*

us the differences between the two oils. The oil that is "beaten for the light" is called *Shemen ha Zayit* or the pure olive oil. The more superior substance of oil, which we will be spending most of our focus on in this section, is called the *Shemen ha Kadosh*, or the "holy anointing oil" *(see Exodus 30:31).*

Our Daily Offering of Oil – *Shemen ha Zayit*

Let's briefly take a look at the pure olive oil and it's importance and application in our lives. First and foremost, the pure olive oil *(Shemen ha Zayit)* is not to be confused with the holy anointing oil *(Shemen ha Kadosh).* The pure olive oil is placed in this text to show us the contrast between the pure olive oil and the *Shemen ha Kadosh*, the holy anointing oil. The pure olive oil had no added element in it and in biblical times was a common commodity used among the people and was used for various purposes. It was something that every home needed. The pure olive oil was used to light the lamps. It was also used to anoint the shields and weapons. In fact, the shields and weapons were only used in battle when they were anointed with this oil. Having this oil on the weapons prophetically parallels how it is only through the anointing that we can wage war.

The pure olive oil was also used for cosmetic purposes. For example, when a person was in mourning after having experienced a death, they would never put oil on their face. But to signify that the mourning had ended they would put the oil on their face. Their faces would then shine and their neighbors would know that they were no longer in mourning.

Beloved, this is, in a sense, a prophetic parallel, because when the anointing is applied to your life, the period of your pain and suffering is over. It is through the anointing that we are delivered from our lives of disappointment and sorrow. These prophetic parallels are extremely so that we might know what the anointing does for every Christian who is willing to activate it.

> *M C +*
>
> *It is through the anointing that we are delivered from our lives of disappointment and sorrow.*

We saw in Exodus 27:20 that every person in Israel had to bring a certain measurement of oil every day. You too, beloved, have the responsibility to offer the oil everyday through your gifts, through your talents, through your abilities, through your sacrifice, and through your service. This is what God wants you to do in His house. The Bible says they were to bring the oil that the lamps may burn continually. That word *burn* in Hebrew is a word, which means *to raise it up*. So this means that every time you apply the oil of the anointing to your life, it causes the flame to be raised to its highest pinnacle of power and purpose. We are not to sit back and hold back our gifts and talents and do nothing with the gifts of the Holy Spirit. Scripture is showing us that this is our obligation; an obligatory offering. This was something that the Lord commanded that Moses order from every child of God that was in the tent of Israel. They had to bring a daily offering of oil and today God wants you to know that the same applies to you. You must bring your daily offering of sacrificial service to God.

MC+

Every time you apply the oil of the anointing to your life, it causes the flame to be raised to its highest pinnacle of power and purpose.

Scripture also shows us that every person who has received Christ has received the anointing.

1 John 2:27 KJV
But the anointing which ye have received of him abideth in you, and ye need not that any man teach you: but as the same anointing teacheth you of all things, and is truth, and is no lie, and even as it hath taught you, ye shall abide in him.

1 John 2:20 KJV
But ye have an unction from the Holy One, and ye know all things.

That word *unction* here when translated from Greek to English is the word for the *anointing*. Meaning that this scripture can be read, *"You have an [anointing] from the Holy One and you know all things."* So every Christian has received the anointing when you receive Christ. There is not some special ceremony that needs to be done for you to receive the anointing. When you receive Jesus you have received the anointing into your life. We need to understand that every Christian has the anointing abiding within them. And we need to understand that every Christian has been called to the anointing. At the heart of the word *Christian* is the word *Christ*. Christ, in Greek is the word *Christos,* which means *The Anointed One*. So your name as a Christian means you *are* an anointed one. Your calling is to the anointing and The One Who *is* anointed lives within you. You have been called to serve God in the anointing. Many are called, but there are few that are chosen. We have discussed the pure olive oil and it's importance and applications in our lives today, now let's take an in depth look at the holy anointing oil or the *Shemen Ha Kadosh.*

The Superior Substance
of the Shemen Ha Kadosh
The Elevating Elements of the Holy Anointing Oil

The Holy Anointing Oil *(Shemen Ha Kadosh)*, unlike the pure olive oil *(Shemen Ha Zayit)*, was given to the prophets to pour upon the kings, high priest, and priests of Israel. It was also used to anoint everything in the tabernacle. Anything that came into the tabernacle was not anointed with the pure olive oil *(Shemen Ha Zayit)* like the shields and weapons were. Quite contrastingly, every vessel that entered the tabernacle was anointed with a superior substance of oil that was only available to the kings and high priests of Israel *(see Exodus 40:9-13)*.

UNDERSTANDING CHEMICAL COMPOUNDS
IN THE ANOINTING

In Exodus 30:22-23 we see that the Lord gave Moses an ointment compound that would be used as a holy anointing oil. This type of oil was created and used for specific purposes. Let's take a look at these verses again.

Exodus 30:22-23a KJV
[22] Moreover the Lord spake unto Moses, saying,
[23] Take thou also unto thee principal spices,

The word *principal* here is the same word that we use for *rosh* in Hebrew. It means *head* or *principal*. There are many reasons why God is commanding Moses to take *principal spices*, which are considered to be the *head* of all the spices at the time. In Biblical times spices had an economic trade value that could be equivocal to our modern day concept of money and the spices used in the *Shemen Ha Kadosh* were of a particularly high value during these times. The types of spices used in this superior substance of oil illustrate the price that is paid through complete surrender to the Spirit in our quest for the anointing.

> *MC+*
> *When the Shemen Ha Kadosh comes upon your life, there is an elevating element within it to make you the head and not the tail, to make you above and not beneath.*

Beloved, when the *Shemen Ha Kadosh* comes upon your life, there is an elevating element within it to make you the head and not the tail, to make you above and not beneath. Correspondingly, there is an elevating property that naturally exists in oil. This is evident whenever you place oil into another liquid substance; the oil always rises to the top. For example, if I have a little glass of water and I pour some oil in it, what's going to happen? The oil is going to rise to the top. Why? Because there is an elevating element that already exists in oil. And when the anointing comes upon your life, there is a power property already available to lift you up above your enemies; to lift you up above every situation; to lift you up above every trial, every tribulation, every sickness, every disease, and everything that you're going through. The anointing breaks the yoke!

"Supernatural Elevation through Constant Consecration to God."

Now the first thing we need to see in this text, in a personal prophetic sense of Scripture, is an anointing compound that can be compared in concept to the chemical language. In Exodus 30, there are symbolic similarities between the concept of chemical language and the supernatural substance in the anointing. In chemistry, a compound is a substance that results in a combination of either two or more chemical elements. Chemistry concerns itself with the property of chemical bonds that are formed between the atoms to create a chemical compound. Most of all the elements on the periodic table and the laws of chemistry were discovered hundreds of years ago. But we are going to see that the Bible already spoke about these types of concepts thousands of years ago. Chemical compounds and everything you need to know about a compound composite has already been given to us in the Word of the living God. We now can begin to understand why the *Shemen Ha Kadosh* differs so much from the

Shemen Ha Zayit, because God instructed Moses to constructed it as a holy ointment compound consisting of many components. Now let's go a little bit deeper to explore what each component was, what measurements of each were used, and the importance of them all.

THE POWER PROPERTIES IN THE ANOINTING

Exodus 30:22-25,31 KJV
[22] Moreover the Lord spake unto Moses, saying, [23] Take thou also unto thee principal spices, of pure myrrh five hundred shekels, and of sweet cinnamon half so much, even two hundred and fifty shekels, and of sweet calamus two hundred and fifty shekels, [24] And of cassia five hundred shekels, after the shekel of the sanctuary, and of oil olive an hin: [25] And thou shalt make it an oil of holy ointment, an ointment compound after the art of the apothecary: it shall be an holy anointing oil. [31] And thou shalt speak unto the children of Israel, saying, This shall be an holy anointing oil unto me throughout your generations.

Myrrh

The first power property that is added to the oil is the essential element of *myrrh*. Myrrh is *the* principal spice. 500 shekels were to be used. Myrrh prophetically parallels the price for the power of God in your life. Myrrh was something that was extremely costly. And there a few accounts in the Bible where myrrh is mentioned being offered or used. For example, after the birth of Jesus we see the kings of the east bringing Him myrrh as a gift. Kings are only going to offer to another King something that is extremely costly. Also, the spikenard that Mary of Bethany used to anoint Jesus with contained elements of myrrh and the Bible tells us that it was very costly. The Bible goes on to give us another example in John 19. When Jesus was being prepared for his burial, Joseph of Arimathea and Nicodemus came with spices and Nicodemus bought one hundred pounds of myrrh to place over the body of Jesus with aloes as they wrapped Him in the linen cloth. And we should take notice that Nicodemus and Joseph of Arimathea were not commoners or average villagers, but instead very wealthy, well-to-do individuals. The cost of myrrh is something extremely expensive. So if it is being used as the principle spice in the compound of the *Shemen Ha Kadosh*, then God is saying, "If you are going to move from the *Shemen Ha Zayit*, the common oil, and move into a round of supernatural status and elevation in the Kingdom of God, then there is a price that needs to be paid for this type of anointing, and that price is your life of sacrifice.

In Addition to containing an elevating property, Myrrh also contains a preservation property. The preservation property is how God or how the anointing will supernaturally sustain and maintain you in a time of test. This means that through everything you're going through in life and through every trial and tribulation you endure, the Power Property of Preservation in the myrrh is going to supernaturally sustain you so that you won't fail.

Jude 1:24 KJV
Now unto him that is able to keep you from falling, and to present you faultless before the presence of his glory with exceeding joy,

1 Peter 1:5 KJV
Who are kept by the power of God through faith unto salvation ready to be revealed in the last time.

MC+
The anointing will keep you during your darkest days. So every time you fall, God is going to pick you up.

The anointing will keep you during your darkest days. So every time you fall, God is going to pick you up. And every time you feel like you can't make it or you feel as if you don't understand what is happening during seemingly chaotic periods in your life, God is going to supernaturally get you to the other side victoriously!

This is what the Shemen Ha Kadosh does. This is what myrrh does. It preserves us. It is a preservative. As mentioned before, myrrh was used to preserve the body of Jesus or anyone you passed away during those times. It was also used for healing. The balm of Gilead was actually composed of myrrh. Myrrh is the Power Property of Preservation in your Tribulation. This is why the Bible says in Isaiah 43:2, *"When thou passest through the waters, I will be with thee; and through the rivers, they shall not overflow thee: when thou walkest through the fire, thou shalt not be burned; neither shall the flame kindle upon thee."*

Beloved, you may be asking yourself, "how"? "How will I have the power to keep going on when I don't feel like I have the strength? How will I have the power to keep serving when I don't feel like serving anymore? How will I have the power to keep saying "yes" to the Lord when I don't want to say yes? Beloved, the answer to these questions is in the element of myrrh found in the anointing. Hallelujah!

Sweet Cinnamon

The second principle spice is the *sweet cinnamon*. The sweet cinnamon does not have as many measurements as myrrh does.

Exodus 30:23a KJV

Take thou also unto thee principal spices, of pure myrrh five hundred shekels, and of sweet cinnamon half so much, even two hundred and fifty shekels...

What is this sweet cinnamon? In Hebrew, The word is for cinnamon is *qinnamon*, which sounds very much like the English word cinnamon. *Qinnamon* is the word that means *to be zealous or to take possession of*. The root of this word *Qinna* not only means to literally be zealous, but also to take possession of something. Beloved, do you need to take possession of a promise? Do you need to take possession of a word? Do you need to take possession of a ministry, or a dream or vision that God has shown you? Scripture is showing us that God has provided the ability to possess every dream, every word, every promise He has ever given us through the element of sweet cinnamon in the anointing. I want you to take possession of every promise God has ever given you, beloved, but you cannot do it without this element in the anointing that will cause you to become zealous enough to boldly take possession of the promises of God!

"You will never be able to fully see your dream or your vision in it's entirety until the anointing of the Shemen ha Kadosh comes on your life."

Now as we take a closer look at the root of the Hebrew word *qinnamon*, we see that *qinna* also means *to redeem or to recover*. Beloved, you may have gone through some tremendously devastating times where you may have lost everything; your hopes, your dreams, your vision, even your possession. Maybe something that you worked years for was gone in a day. People, maybe even those closest to you, may have disappointed or hurt you so deeply that you wonder if you'll ever be able to get your joy or peace back. But I'm here to tell you, dear one, that there is an answer from the Lord. You can get it all back. You can make a miraculous comeback. And this can all be done through the anointing. The element of sweet cinnamon in the anointing will cause you to be able to recover everything that the enemy has stolen out of your life.

> *MC+*
> *You can make a miraculous comeback. And this can all be done through the anointing.*

Sweet Calamus

The third ingredient in this compound composite that we see is the *sweet calamus* or sweet cane in Hebrew.

Exodus 30:23b KJV
And of sweet calamus two hundred and fifty shekels...

It was a special spice from Arabia during biblical times. But the cane or the sweet cane was also known as a *reed*. Reeds were used for taking measurements in the Bible. If you look in the book of Ezekiel, beginning in the 40th chapter, Ezekiel begins to have the vision of the third temple. During this vision, everything was measured by reeds. Reeds were used to measure the walls and even everything placed inside of the temple like the Ark of the Covenant, all of the vessels, and holy things were measured using reeds. You may be asking yourself, "That sounds very interesting Dr. Corral, but what does that have to do with me and my destiny?" Beloved, it has everything to do with your destiny. This means that there are certain things that you have been specifically anointed to do, that nobody else can do. And there is an unlimited parameter in that area of your expertise that God has given you. For instance, you can take a certain area that God has given you, and you can bring that measurement to another level. It can be expanded out and there can be an *extension into another dimension* of anointing and power in that gift. This is the Power Property of sweet calamus found in the *Shemen ha Kadosh*.

> *MC+*
>
> *There are certain things that you have been specifically anointed to do, that nobody else can do. And there is an unlimited parameter in that area of your expertise that God has given you.*

Beloved, you don't have to stay stuck where you were five years ago. You can take your gift into another place, into another realm that nobody else has ever taken that gift to before! It is time for us all to go to the next level! If you are a singer, if you are a preacher, if you are an intercessor, it is time to expand the parameters of your gifting and bring that measurement to another level. But the ability to expand and to go to a higher level and to not stay stuck at the level you currently are, can only come through the anointing; not through your works, not through your talents, not through any earthly abilities you may possess. It can only come through the anointing of the *Shemen Ha Kadosh* on our lives through the help of the Holy Spirit.

Cassia

The fourth and final power property in the anointing, is *Cassia*.

Exodus 30:24 KJV
And of cassia five hundred shekels, after the shekel of the sanctuary, and of oil olive an hin:

Cassia, in a literal sense, is made from little pieces of bark from trees found in Arabia. They are rolled up and ground into powder. But in Hebrew the verb *cassia* means *to kindle with fire, to strike it with fire, or to be entangled with the fire*. Just as with myrrh, God wants 500 shekels of cassia to compose this compound. Why? Because scripture is showing us the importance of having your anointing consumed with the fire of God. And not just any type of fire, but the purifying properties of fire. Fire not only purifies, but it also brings things into a place of excellence. Through the element of cassia, the perfecting properties of excellence and elegance are released into your life. When the cassia is released into your life, you will desire to do everything in an excellent way. Why? Because the fire will purify and perfect your gift in such a way that it will be brought up to a level of kingly excellence.

Psalm 45:8 KJV
All thy garments smell of myrrh, and aloes, and cassia, out of the ivory palaces, whereby they have made thee glad.

Beloved, when the anointing of the *Shemen Ha Kadosh* comes upon you, there is a supernatural substance of fire through the element of cassia that will come into your being. It will not only to bring you up to a new place of excellence, but it will also purify your thoughts, your actions, and your character. Miraculous transformations occur in our lives because of the myrrh, because of the sweet calamus, because of the sweet cinnamon, and because of the cassia. Each of these elements in the *Shemen Ha Kadosh* are essential to the anointing in our lives and are given to us for consecration and dedication in service to God. They separate us from what is secular so that we may be used for the glory of God!

HOW WE ARE CHOSEN BY GOD

Beloved, I would like to briefly share with you how God elects and selects for the purposes of the anointing. The first thing we need to do when reading Scripture is to discover what the author's intent in writing a particular passage is; even if it is a narrative.

As we look at 1 Samuel 16, it is clear that this particular narrative pertains to the anointing of King David. But throughout this narrative there is a high emphasis on the process of elimination. We see one brother after another being presented to the Prophet Samuel. But the author, who happens to be the prophet Samuel himself, goes out of his way to show us men who, in the natural, seem to be highly qualified and seem to possess stellar attributes. They had the looks. They had the talent. They possessed extraordinary abilities. But there is a blatant repetitiveness implemented throughout these verses so that we don't miss the intent of the author to show us that these individuals are being disqualified from their destinies. There is a clear evaluation and the process of elimination taking place. Let's take a look at the text.

Dr. Michelle Corral

1 Samuel 16:1 KJV
And the Lord said unto Samuel, How long wilt thou mourn
for Saul, seeing I have rejected him from reigning over
Israel? fill thine horn with oil, and go, I will send thee to
Jesse the Bethlehemite: for I have provided me a king
among his sons.

Out of the sons of Jesse one of them is going to be selected
as the next king of Israel. So the Prophet Samuel travels to
Jesse's home and instructs him to bring all his sons to the
banquet table. There he will inquire of the Lord, which son
will be king. Instead of simply telling us who was elected,
Scripture blatantly goes out of its way to show us how each
son was rejected. Let's look at verses 6 and 7.

1 Samuel 16:6-7a KJV
[6] And it came to pass, when they were come, that he
looked on Eliab, and said, Surely the Lord's anointed is
before him. [7] But the Lord said unto Samuel, Look not on
his countenance, or on the height of his stature; because I
have refused him:

The message one could take from these verses that are
showing us the person being disqualified is that this is just
a matter of Samuel having the right discernment to see
whom God has chosen. But Scripture then goes on to show
us yet another individual who is being excluded through
the process of elimination. An important fact we must

constantly be aware of, beloved, is that this word is not written simply as a historical narrative. It is written in the Word so that we might understand the author's intent to reveal to us how God very specifically selects individuals for His purposes. Let's take a look at another individual.

1 Samuel 16:8-10 KJV
[8] Then Jesse called Abinadab, and made him pass before Samuel. And he said, Neither hath the Lord chosen this. [9] Then Jesse made Shammah to pass by. And he said, Neither hath the Lord chosen this. [10] Again, Jesse made seven of his sons to pass before Samuel. And Samuel said unto Jesse, The Lord hath not chosen these.

We see the Prophet Samuel revealing that yet another son has been rejected by God. This, beloved, seems to be a little bit out of character. When studying Torah, a concept in Hebrew you will see frequently is the concept of *middot* or character trait. One of the primary negative character traits that a person can possess is to shame someone else. To be in alignment with Torah teachings, one is not going to publicly say, "The Lord has not chosen you," because this would cause the other person shame and possibly damage their reputation. So it seems a bit out of the ordinary and very contradictory for the Prophet Samuel, who knows Torah Law, to repetitively and very blatantly show us each son that was rejected by God. But what we need to understand, is that the Prophet Samuel is purposefully using this literary technique to show us that God did not deem these individuals as qualified based solely on their gifts, their talents, their good looks, their position in the family, or their status or popularity in the community. God's criteria for election are vastly different from that of man's.

ℳℭ+
The one you never expected is the one God elected.

The one you never expected is the one God elected.

1 Samuel 16:11 KJV
And Samuel said unto Jesse, Are here all thy children? And he said, There remaineth yet the youngest, and, behold, he keepeth the sheep. And Samuel said unto Jesse, Send and fetch him: for we will not sit down till he come hither.

Now, you must understand, beloved, that the Bible is inerrant. The Bible is infallible. It is absolutely without error. Scripture is completely sufficient. We do not need another Bible. We do not need the book of Mormon. We do not need revelations that somebody got to add to the scripture. Everything is completely impeccable in the word of God. There's no higher authority than the word of God. However, sometimes translators can misinterpret a meaning because they have multiple meanings in Hebrew. And you can take a word and translate it, but actually misinterpret it altogether. It doesn't mean that the Bible is wrong, it just means that the translators did not accurately translate that particular word correctly possibly due to their lack in understanding the culture, the language, or ancient biblical customs.

In this text the word *youngest* is not the most accurate choice of words. The original language (Hebrew) says *"there remaineth yet the [kattan]."* What is a *kattan*? One of the meanings of the *kattan* in Hebrew is *little*. But if a person does not quite understand the culture or the language, then one may mistake the word *little* for *young or youngest*. And certainly *young* is one of the translations of the word *kattan*. However, there are other Hebrew words that provide a much more accurate translation for the word *young*. *Kattan* in this verse does not mean *young* but instead means *lesser* or *insignificant*.

Let's take a moment to evaluate the context of this section of scripture. During this time in Biblical history, it would be a great honor to have the prophet come to your house for dinner. You would make sure everyone knew that you would be entertaining such a distinguished guest. The fact that Jesse did not invite all his sons and for him not to even consider extending the invitation to David is unfathomable. Another fact to take into consideration during our evaluation is Jesse's socio-economic status. Jesse was an extremely wealthy man. He was the descendent and grandson of Boaz. He, in turn, inherited all the wealth of Boaz. Verse 11 revealed to us that David was made to keep the sheep, but during biblical times only men who were paupers used their children as shepherds. Being a shepherd was considered the lowest of jobs.

David's father and his brothers tried to disqualify him from the selection process, but God had different plans. Instead, David's brothers themselves ended up being disqualified through the process of elimination. Someone who they all never expected and who was made to do such an undesirable job was selected and elected by God to be the next king of Israel. Someone who man had rejected, God elected! When Samuel instructed them to bring David in, he took the horn of oil, and he anointed David in the presence of his brothers and his father. So when we read Psalm 23, we now know what David was referring to.

Psalm 23:5 KJV
Thou preparest a table before me in the presence of mine enemies: thou anointest my head with oil; my cup runneth over.

Beloved, if you have always been ashamed of being the *kattan* and have always felt worthless; if you have always felt as if you had nothing to offer, then today is your day to know that all of this is the very criterion of your call. The things you despised the most about yourself or your current situation are the very things that are going to open the doors of destiny in your life.

Prayer

Wonderful Holy Spirit, I offer myself as a living sacrifice. I'm willing to pay the price for the anointing in my life. I ask for the anointing to take me to another level. I want my gift to be brought to its highest pinnacle of purpose and power. I ask You to deposit the myrrh within me and preserve me. Deposit the sweet cinnamon. Give me the power to possess the promises. Dear God, deposit the sweet cane in my life. Stretch me into my new anointing. I ask You Wonderful Lord to bring the Power of the Spirit through the cassia. Let me be empowered with the purifying properties of the anointing in the Mighty Name of Jesus, Amen.

Dr. Michelle Corral

Chesed Publishing

What is Chesed?

Chesed means "loving kindness" in Hebrew. Our publication house is called Chesed Publishing because when you purchase a book, you are helping us to do the impossible for people that could never help themselves.

We provide daily feeding programs to orphans and grandmothers, pay for educational fees for children in our orphan homes, conduct medical missions throughout the world, purchase clean water wells, and so much more.

In April 2016, Chesed Publishing was founded to financially support Dr. Michelle Corral's vision of acts of chesed to the poor, along with the mission to pass on the wealth of teaching that God entrusted to her to the next generation.

Books Authored by Dr. Michelle Corral

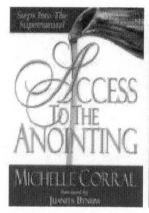

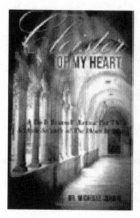
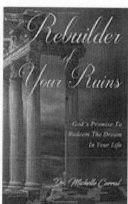

For a Complete List of CDs and Ministry Resources

Contact:

Breath of the Spirit Prophetic Word Center
P.O. BOX 2676
Orange, CA 92859

Phone # (714) 694-1100

Youtube.com/DrMichelleCorral
Word Network on Mondays
@ 10:30 pm PST
www.breathofthespirit.org
www.drmichellecorral.com
facebook.com/Dr.Corral